TRIUMPH OF THE
WALKING DEAD

OTHER SMART POP TELEVISION AND COMICS TITLES

Batman Unauthorized
Boarding the Enterprise
Farscape Forever!
Finding Serenity
Five Seasons of Angel
Fringe Science
Inside Joss' Dollhouse
King Kong Is Back!
The Man from Krypton
The Psychology of Joss Whedon
The Psychology of Superheroes
Serenity Found
Seven Seasons of Buffy
So Say We All
Star Wars on Trial
Stepping Through the Stargate
Taking the Red Pill
A Taste of True Blood
The Unauthorized X-Men
A Visitor's Guide to Mystic Falls
Webslinger

OTHER ANTHOLOGIES EDITED BY JAMES LOWDER

Astounding Hero Tales
The Best of All Flesh
The Book of All Flesh
The Book of Final Flesh
The Book of More Flesh
Curse of the Full Moon
The Doom of Camelot
Family Games: The 100 Best
Hobby Games: The 100 Best
Legends of the Pendragon
Path of the Bold
Path of the Just
Realms of Infamy
Realms of Valor
Worlds of Their Own

TRIUMPH OF THE
WALKING DEAD

ROBERT KIRKMAN'S ZOMBIE EPIC ON PAGE AND SCREEN

EDITED BY
JAMES LOWDER

AN IMPRINT OF BENBELLA BOOKS, INC. DALLAS, TEXAS

Triumph of The Walking Dead © 2011 by James Lowder

Smart Pop is an Imprint of BenBella Books, Inc.
10300 N. Central Expressway, Suite 400
Dallas, TX 75231
www.benbellabooks.com
www.smartpopbooks.com
Send feedback to feedback@benbellabooks.com

Printed in the United States of America
10 9 8 7 6 5 4 3 2 1

Library of Congress Cataloging-in-Publication Data
Triumph of the walking dead : Robert Kirkman's zombie epic on page and screen / edited by James Lowder.
p. cm.
Includes bibliographical references and index.
ISBN 978-1-936661-13-8 (alk. paper)
1. Kirkman, Robert. Walking dead. 2. Walking dead (Television program) 3. Graphic novels—United States. 4. Zombies in literature. I. Lowder, James.
PN6727.K586W338 2011
741.5'973—dc23
2011029085

Copyediting by Rebecca Logan and Oriana Leckert
Proofreading by Nora Nussbaum
Cover design by Kit Sweeney
Cover and interior artwork © 2011 Rafael Kayanan
Text design and composition by Neuwirth & Associates, Inc.
Printed by Bang Printing

Distributed by Perseus Distribution
http://www.perseusdistribution.com/

PERMISSIONS

{ CONTENTS }

THE WALKING DEAD, WITH ENTOURAGE

Dead folk won't stay dead.

They keep getting up.

Least they do in fiction and film. They come out of the grave, or roll off the slab, and head out for breakfast, lunch, dinner, and any available snack in between. They do this without need of reservations, manners, or even a table and chair, and one can certainly dismiss the tablecloth. They grab the living and eat them up, and readers and viewers keep paying to eat that experience up right with them.

Year after year after year.

It's hard to explain why the dead won't die, why they just keep coming back, filling books and stories and comics, shambling across big screens and TV sets, even popping up in poems and car commercials.

What's up?

The idea isn't really new, though different writers and filmmakers have refined it over the years. In fact, it goes way back. If memory serves me, and it may not, there's a line in *Gilgamesh,* the oldest written story we know of, about the hungry dead, how they will come back from hell, or its equivalent, to smack teeth on raw flesh.

So, the idea of someone dead getting a ticket back to the land of the living so he might consume the flesh of the living has been floating around for a long time. For that matter, some Christian religious rituals involve consuming the Savior. The wine and wafer is interpreted as being, at the moment of the rite, the literal flesh and blood of Jesus.

Kind of creepy, really.

But what exactly is it that keeps these dead folk staggering back?

What holds our interest?

What is it in our subconscious that wants them to flail about, grab and bite, smack and chew?

Answers abound, and all of them are probably right, at least on some level. The simplest boils down to this: It's the End of the World, and there's monsters out there. You could substitute a variety of monsters, I suppose. It's just that right now the monsters happen to be the dead. And when you look closely, those zombies can easily be metaphors for disease, terrorism, conservatism and conformity, liberalism and anarchy. They can represent our natural fear of things that are dead and will get stink on us, and they can remind us of our ultimate fate, no matter what future plans we've made. They can even force us to confront the taboo of cannibalism, while we're at it.

What these walking dead are supposed to represent is a long damn list, and again, any and all of the items on that list, from certain points of view, can be accurate. The articles in this book explore at least a few of them in far more detail.

But it's not the number of things zombies stand for that explains the appeal of the graphic novel and the recent AMC series *The Walking Dead*. It's not the scares, either.

The dead are creepy, for sure, but what makes this series in both mediums so strong—so convincing that it allows us to eagerly suspend our disbelief of something we know is frankly impossible—is this: the living characters are so believable. Because of that, we are more willing to embrace the concept that the dead can walk and eat—and if they don't eat you, just bite you, then you too are infected and have a rabid desire to consume human flesh.

If you believe the characters in a story, you will believe most anything. It's the key to making a good fantasy work. Make all the day-to-day details, the lives and interests of the characters, real, and we'll accept those zombies, or aliens, or vampires, or werewolves.

The Walking Dead is full of real characters. The good, the bad, the ugly, and mostly, the complex: that's what keeps pulling us back. We want to see how things turn out for these folks— some of them because we like them, some because we don't like them. Others because we are at least curious about them or find them interesting.

Another thing that is so intriguing about the series is that TV has mainstreamed zombies. Once, this sort of thing was the subject of second-rate comic books and no-budget films starring any warm body willing to show up. Now it's on a mainstream television channel. That which was once thought of as gross and taboo is now weekly fodder for the family, to be watched between bites of popcorn and slurps of a soda pop.

The idea that you can tune into the American Movie Classics channel and see something formerly thought of as only for fringe outlets is especially inviting to someone like me who, growing up, had only three heavily censored network channels. I hated watching movies, especially horror movies, translated to TV, because they were ripped apart, bleeped, voiced-over, or shown late at night when the networks hoped that the bulk of the population would be asleep.

But let's get to the important part.

This book.

If you're a fan of the *Walking Dead* comics or the TV show, or both, or if you're just curious and want to get your feet wet in the zombie craze, this book is unequivocally the place to start. It is chock-full of zombie goodness and discusses the series and the characters and the zombie craze in far greater and more interesting detail than I attempt in this brief introduction.

So, I leave you now.

The world has gone wonkers.

The hungry dead are out there.

And they're looking for you.

Watch yourself.

Joe R. Lansdale
Nacogdoches, Texas

The *New York Times Book Review* describes JOE R. LANSDALE as a writer with "a folklorist's eye for telling detail and a front-porch raconteur's sense of pace." Lansdale is the author of thirty novels and over two hundred short stories, articles, and essays. His work has received an Edgar, two *New York Times* Notable Books, seven Bram Stoker Awards, the British Fantasy Award, the Inkpot Award, the Herodotus Award for historical fiction, and many others. His novella "Bubba Ho-Tep" was made into a cult movie of the same name. His work has also been filmed for Showtime. His latest novel is *Devil Red*, published by Knopf. Online at joerlansdale.com.

IN MEDIAS APOCALYPSIS

All zombies are created equal. That's kind of their thing.

Sure, you may be able to spot little differences. One may haul around the teddy bear it cherished when it was still a little girl, while another may wear the remnants of its nun's habit or its softball league uniform. They can be differentiated by the number of limbs still attached to their torsos or by their movement predilections—fast or slow, roamers or lurkers. In the end, though, the classic zombie is just a hungry mouth in search of the next bite of warm flesh.

Writers sometimes cheat a bit and grant their living dead a measure of residual intelligence. Fair enough. The best way to explore what makes a zombie a zombie is to push the boundaries, and tropes can, and should, evolve. Even the brain-munching, virus-spreading machine that has come to embody the term "zombie" in the twenty-first century had a twentieth-century predecessor in the will-bereft slaves introduced to Western pop culture in 1929 through W.B. Seabrook's Haitian travelogue *The Magic Island* and, a few years later, the low-budget Bela Lugosi classic *White Zombie* (1932). George Romero changed all that. With 1968's *Night of the Living Dead* he transformed the sad victims robbed of their souls through sorcery or chemistry into hyper-aggressive monsters. Since that landmark moment in cinematic horror, we've come to expect our zombies to seek out and devour the living, who, once fallen, will then join the relentless, hunger-fueled ranks of the undead.

Zombies in the Romero style are precisely what Robert Kirkman delivered when he kicked off the comic book series *The Walking Dead* in 2003. The first few issues tread other rather familiar patches of storytelling ground, too. The opening, where Rick Grimes wakes up in the hospital only to discover the world has gone to hell in his absence, has been criticized as being derivative of the film *28 Days Later* (2002). It *is* derivative, but not of Danny Boyle's film, which premiered in the United States after work on the first issue of the *Walking Dead* comic had wrapped. Both Kirkman and Boyle were tapping into a long tradition in postapocalyptic fiction of hospitalized or otherwise incapacitated protagonists awakening to a world ravaged by a weird menace, a tradition that includes John Wyndham's classic *The Day of the Triffids* (1951) and the far less familiar, wonderfully pulpy *Vampires Overhead* (1935) by Alan Hyder. (In the latter, the heroes miss the invasion of the space vampires because they're sleeping off a drunk in a brewery's underground tunnels.) As with his unashamedly Romero-inspired zombies, Kirkman is utilizing very familiar narrative elements here.

When I reviewed the first dozen or so issues of *The Walking Dead* back in 2004 for the late, lamented *Amazing Stories*, I noted the predictability of the opening story arc, but also commented how the comics were building momentum and had the potential to move beyond their inspirations. If you consider "momentum" to mean an Eisner Award for "Best Continuing Series," an incredibly successful television show, and a flood of licensed merchandise—everything from board and video games to novels, T-shirts, action figures, lighters, and mugs—then I guess you could say I called that bit right.

The truth is, though, no one outside of Kirkman and the team working with him to create the original *Walking Dead* comics could have guessed where those earliest issues might lead. The heart of the series, the thing that makes it so compulsively readable and so emotionally involving—the characters—had yet to be fully formed. They remain works in progress even now. Only Kirkman knows if Rick will turn out to be a hero, the founder of a new human civilization, or a villain, a scarred monster like the Governor, for whom the ends justify the most brutal of means, particularly when it comes to his child. Or perhaps Rick's fate is that of the archetypal Western lawman: to be able to travel between the wild world and the civilized one—the domains of Chaos and Order—but unable to find a permanent home in either.

You might think that uncertainty would be a disadvantage to commentators, but just the opposite is true. The evolving nature of the characters and their changing relationship to the harsh, zombie-plagued world provide readers with a near-endless source of fodder for debate, and the uncertainty only makes that debate all the more lively. Unlike so many serial narratives, where the heroes are fixed points, unaffected by the furious adventures spinning around them, *The Walking Dead* features protagonists who are most assuredly altered by their experiences. And Kirkman has shown time and again that those transformations will be dramatic—and deserving of serious discussion. The point of this essay collection is to showcase some of those discussions, to share some of the lively debates inspired by *The Walking Dead*, in both its comic book and television incarnations.

This book itself came about, as sometimes happens in publishing, from an offhand comment. Smart Pop editor-in-chief Leah Wilson and I were exchanging emails about another project when I noted that *The Walking Dead* was worthy of a collection and that, if they pursued the project, I'd love to write something for it. Over the years I've written a lot about the living dead. They regularly pop up in my novels, short stories, and comic book scripts. I've reviewed dozens of zombie films and books, and included them in the curriculum when I've had the opportunity to teach about cinema or pop culture. I've also edited several volumes of zombie-themed short stories—the Books of Flesh anthology series, which started with *The Book of All Flesh* back in 2001, a couple years before the current Zombie Renaissance kicked off.

You can see where this is going. After a few more emails, Leah suggested that I might be the right wrangler for this zombie-fest. Things progressed quickly from there. I'd already come up with a mental list of writers whose opinions on *The Walking Dead* I wanted to hear. It hadn't been hard to do. Books and articles by the authors included in these pages crowd the shelves in my office, and the websites for which they write are bookmarked on my browser. If you're a zombiephile, or just a devotee of well-written pop-culture criticism, you should recognize their names, too.

The authors had access to the comics through the end of the epic "No Way Out" story arc, and to the first season of the television show. So we're commenting on the apocalypse, and the protagonists' reaction to it, while it's still going on. The essays inspired by that material include several on Rick Grimes from writers promoting perspectives—often contrasting or even contradictory ones—exploring his actions and, yes, suggesting his possible fate. Other pieces offer competing views on the mythic and archetypal aspects of the series, the ultimate meaning or meaninglessness of the zombie resurrections, as well as *The Walking Dead*'s place in the history of horror comics and the ways in which changing media usage impacts the audience's reaction to the gruesomeness and gore on the TV show. More than anything, though, the essays collected between these covers reveal just some of the many reasons the important writers and scholars participating in this volume find *The Walking Dead* worth such careful study.

So barricade the doors and windows and join some veterans of the zombie apocalypse around the failing light as they share their thoughts on Robert Kirkman's blood-soaked masterpiece.

All zombies are created equal.

All zombie stories are not.

The best ones, like *The Walking Dead*, get into your head and make you think—make you fatten up the gray matter that the living dead lust after so ravenously.

James Lowder
New Berlin, Wisconsin

TRIUMPH OF THE
WALKING DEAD

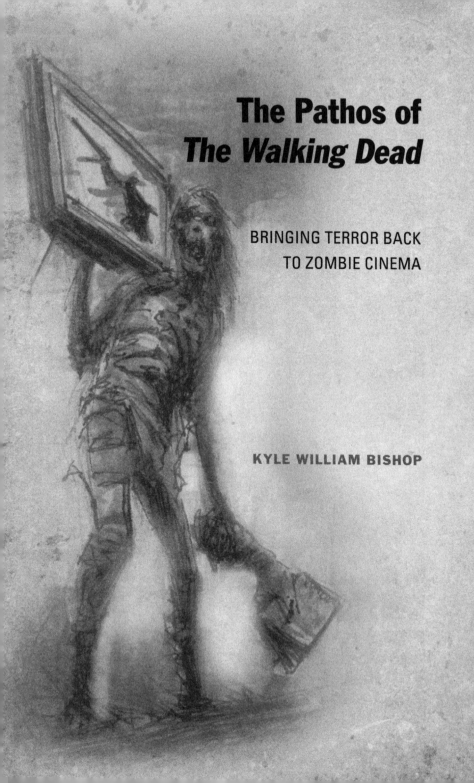

The Pathos of
The Walking Dead

BRINGING TERROR BACK
TO ZOMBIE CINEMA

KYLE WILLIAM BISHOP

n his introduction to the first trade paperback collection of the comic book series *American Vampire* (2010), Stephen King laments the state of vampire mythology in contemporary popular culture:

> Here's what vampires shouldn't be: pallid detectives who drink Bloody Marys and only work at night; lovelorn southern gentlemen; anorexic teenage girls; boy-toys with big dewy eyes.
>
> What should they be?
>
> Killers, honey. Stone killers who never get enough of that tasty Type-A. Bad boys and girls. Hunters. In other words, Midnight America. Red, white and blue, accent on the red. Those vamps got hijacked by a lot of soft-focus romance.

The man speaks some hard truths, and here's where my concerns come in: zombies are suffering a similar treatment. Ever since Danny Boyle kicked off Hollywood's Zombie Renaissance with *28 Days Later* in 2002, pop culture has been flooded with zombie stories of all stripes. Sadly, many of these feature lame parody, excessive cliché, and illogical changes to the subgenre. The problem? Too many zombies just aren't frightening anymore; in fact, they've even become bizarrely lovable, showing up at festive "zombie walks," being sold as plush dolls and children's toys, starring as revisionist superheroes in the Marvel Zombies series, and even appearing as the sympathetic leads in popular romantic fiction, as in S.G. Browne's 2009 novel *Breathers: A Zombie's Lament*. But zombies used to be *scary*, right?

Luckily for fans who recognize, and perhaps already miss, the visceral power of the living dead, Frank Darabont is working hard to remind viewers that zombies are fundamentally terrifying. His new television show, *The Walking Dead*, adapted from Robert Kirkman's smash comic book series, reinvigorates the cinematic zombie narrative, using both gravitas and pathos to restore fear to the subgenre. Drawing on the key dramatic lesson of George A. Romero's foundational *Dawn of the Dead* (1978), Darabont knows the only way a zombie can frighten an otherwise benumbed audience—especially in this era of oversaturation and parody—is if the viewers actually *care* about the human characters. Following Kirkman's lead, Darabont makes the living protagonists the undisputed stars of *The Walking Dead*, but he uses the cinematic medium to increase the tragedy of his characters by making viewers really fear *for* them—and, by cathartic extension, makes the audience experience their terror firsthand.

Noël Carroll's insightful analysis of how art-horror functions on a physical as well as a psychological level is as relevant today as when he first published *The Philosophy of Horror* more than twenty years ago. In his application of Aristotle's conception of catharsis, Carroll emphasizes how consumers of the horror genre literally experience the emotions represented by the dramatic production. The audience actually *feels* something during horror, and these psychological and physiological responses parallel those experienced by the depicted characters, creating the mirroring effect that defines the genre. Carroll points out that unlike other modes of fiction, such as classical tragedy, in which the viewer "safely" and indirectly experiences emotions as a matter of artistic verisimilitude, horror manifests actual *physical* symptoms, be they shuddering, tingling, trembling, nausea, or even involuntary screaming. In other words, viewers don't simply get over being scared just because they know they're watching an actor simulating a terrified response; audience members must deal with the unpleasant physical reactions themselves.

But how can simulated emotions become real for an audience? According to Carroll, the two crucial components of effective art-horror are implicit impurity and a perceived threat. For virtually all zombie narratives, a visceral sense of impurity—what Julia Kristeva famously describes in 1982's *Powers of Horror* as the "abject"—is ubiquitous. After all, zombies are rotting, decaying, and, more often than not, violently disfigured corpses. Viewers cannot avoid revulsion when confronted by the physical defilement and morbidity of the zombie, and this reaction against such impurity constitutes half of the subgenre's effectiveness. However, Carroll underscores how impurity alone would result only in the emotion of disgust, not fear; for audiences to experience the physical and psychological gamut of horror, the monster or situation must also be inherently dangerous. Thanks to the mirroring effect of art-horror, when a narrative demonstrates a physical threat against a character, viewers perceive this threat to be directed at themselves as well. However, I argue that audience members perceive the threat this way only when they see those imperiled characters in powerfully sympathetic terms.

For zombie stories to evoke real fear in their consumers, authors, directors, and actors must use the rhetorical appeal of pathos to encourage an empathetic reaction. Such an emotional connection with the heroes of a zombie narrative is certainly nothing new. Romero made human relationships, audience connectivity, and emotional bonding the key components of *Dawn of the Dead*. Indeed, the opening shot of the film introduces viewers intimately to the vulnerable Fran. Presented in close-up, Fran awakens from a terrible nightmare to find herself embroiled in an even more terrifying reality: the dead have risen and are feeding on the living. The entire movie is thus Fran's story, the chronicle of her struggles both to survive and to protect her unborn child. If anything, the zombies are mere plot devices to this central human story. Although *Dawn of the Dead* begins with substantial action and carnage, once the four beleaguered survivors of the assault find the abandoned Monroeville Mall, the story shifts to a psychological emphasis, charting their efforts at re-creating a social, even familial, community.

With the story moved to the relative safety of the mall, the pace of the narrative slows dramatically, allowing the audience time to get to know the four characters on a personal level: Roger, a trigger-happy SWAT member who relishes killing zombies; Peter, his level-headed and loyal friend and colleague; Stephen, a brash chopper pilot who revels in the materialistic gluttony the mall offers; and, of course, Fran, who grows increasingly sympathetic as her due date approaches. Over the course of the film, viewers cheer the heroes' successful efforts to convert the mall into a hideout and proxy home. They share the glee with which the men rob a bank to use the worthless cash for their high-stakes poker games, laugh as the quartet try on increasingly ridiculous outfits, and feel Fran's emptiness when she refuses to take Stephen's proffered engagement ring. Rather than making these protagonists into superheroes or larger-than-life survivalists, Romero shows them to be fallible and flawed human beings—but nonetheless charismatic and likable.

Yet the power of *Dawn of the Dead* comes not only from the amicable nature of these characters but also from the various tragedies that befall each of them. After Roger is bitten by a zombie, viewers must watch the slow and painful advance of the infection, sitting by helplessly as the once-vibrant man grows pale and weak. Peter's diligent deathbed vigil evokes the audience's own sense of pity, and they observe with growing horror as Peter must ultimately execute the zombie his friend has become. Stephen's death proves no less ghastly, as he is brutally killed by a gang of zombies that trap him in an elevator. When he emerges shortly thereafter, covered in wounds and pale from blood loss, viewers feel sorrow for both him and Fran. Such personalized depictions of pain and suffering enhance the cathartic experience of the audience, for as Aristotle explains in *On Rhetoric*, "such things are necessarily causes of fear as seem to have great potential for destruction or for causing harms that lead to great pains." The carnage of *Dawn of the Dead* becomes more than mere screen violence. Because the audience views the characters as living, breathing humans, they see Roger, Peter, Stephen, and Fran's suffering in precisely the terms Aristotle singles out: *harm* and *pain*.

Clearly, art-horror must forge emotional connections between viewers and the depicted characters for the audience to feel fear. Unfortunately, this reliance on pathos has been increasingly lost, forgotten, or at least neglected in many zombie narratives. Even Romero has largely abandoned this focal point, as can be seen in *Survival of the Dead* (2009). In stark contrast to *Dawn of the Dead*, Romero's most recent zombie movie opens with a close-up of the hardened and stoic Sergeant "Nicotine" Crockett. Nothing about his appearance is approachable or inviting, and even though he tells viewers in voice-over how zombies are only hard to kill when they were once friends, he soon shoots a number of his infected platoon members with cold impassivity. Crockett and his gang are self-described "lousy people" who seem to kill more humans than zombies, AWOL vigilantes engaged in petty theft. The group's lone female member, a stereotyped Latina lesbian known simply as "Tomboy," perceptively points out,

"All the wrong people are dying. Seems like all we got left are assholes." She isn't wrong; the embarrassingly generic Irishmen of Plum Island are similarly unlikable. The hip flask–carrying Patrick O'Flynn has decided "the living would be better off if the dead stayed dead," but he fights living and dead alike with equal amounts of heartless brutality.

Throughout the course of *Survival of the Dead*, the two emotional responses required for catharsis, pity and fear, are notably absent. It's hard to feel anything when Kenny is shot and killed, despite Crockett's uncharacteristic emotional reaction, and viewers are unlikely moved when "Soldier Zombie," "Hot-Headed Good Old Boy," or "Fisherman" die either—or when "Boy" and "Tomboy" survive, for that matter—because the audience hasn't been given the chance to get to know them or to recognize them as real people. In fact, none of the characters are more than surface types, too interchangeable and thinly developed to matter at all, so their deaths create no sense of loss for the audience. Fear is even more overtly absent from the film. When Crockett is surprised by a zombie on the ferryboat, he doesn't react with fear at all; if anything, he's simply annoyed. On the island, the deadhead "cattle" prove to be little threat and certainly no cause for Seamus Muldoon to be afraid. He shoots them with casual disregard, offhandedly describing the trouble as being "no more than usual." About halfway through the movie, Muldoon justifies his callous murder of refugee humans by calling them "strangers—no kin of mine," and that's ultimately the problem with the whole film. The depicted humans remain strangers to the end, and viewers just can't feel anything approaching pity or fear for them.

Unfortunately, *Survival of the Dead* fails to deliver a cathartic horror experience. But this conclusion should come as no surprise to the careful viewer. After all, Crockett tells the audience via voice-over in the film's first scene that "the dead were coming back to life. We should've been afraid of them, but . . . we weren't." This declaration says it all—the zombies of *Survival of the Dead* aren't particularly frightening, not because they are easy to kill, as Crockett claims, but because the audience cannot find any reason to care for the film's protagonists. By not having someone to fear *for*, viewers have no reason to fear at all. Ultimately, Romero's latest zombie film relies more on shock and surprise than it does on any sophisticated development of pathos. Carroll dismisses from the ranks of true horror narratives stories that rely solely on surprising viewers with loud noises, startling movements, and unexpected action because "horror is not reducible to this sort of shock." Quality art-horror produces emotional responses, not merely knee-jerk reactions caused by being startled.

The Walking Dead, on the other hand, effectively uses pathos to reaffirm the zombie narrative's place in the cinematic art-horror tradition. The enterprise began in 2003, when Kirkman launched his comic book series to expand on the limited scope of existing zombie movies. As he explains in the introduction to *The Walking Dead: Days Gone Bye*, the first trade paperback collection of the comics series, "The worst part of every zombie movie is the end. I always want to know what happens next . . . I just want it to keep going." In other words, it's largely about duration—a serialized narrative can develop a much longer story arc than a 120-minute movie. Such a broad narrative canvas provides room for expansive action, as well as long-term and detailed character development. This concentration, one that shifts focus away from the grisly monsters and onto the besieged human survivors, has now been realized even more effectively on the small screen. Darabont comments on this power of the series in a recent *Entertainment Weekly* interview

("The Walking Dead"): "It's more about the characters than the zombies . . . This is about a group of people who are forced to survive together, be a family together, and endure very, very difficult circumstances." Season one has already proven Darabont's assertions, as the real story of *The Walking Dead* is one of family and similar social relationships.

Indeed, zombies are often conspicuously absent from the screen version of *The Walking Dead*, marginalized to the benefit of the human characters. The initial shots of the pilot emphasize Deputy Rick Grimes, and although viewers do see a zombie before they hear a word of spoken dialogue, the creature doesn't appear until three full minutes into the cold opening. As in the graphic novel, in which Kirkman's first thirty-one panels are completely zombie free, Darabont's zombies take their time showing up in this first episode. No zombies are depicted in the series' opening credit sequence, which shows instead images of apocalyptic devastation and broken picture frames with photos that introduce the show's human protagonists. After the opening credits, the initial story focuses exclusively on Rick and his backstory—with almost fourteen minutes passing before any sign of zombies appears at all. Despite the pilot episode's thrilling and admittedly shocking climax, in which hundreds of hungry zombies swarm the tank in which Rick is hiding, "Days Gone Bye" (1-1) has less than seventeen minutes of footage depicting the walking dead—which is only about a fourth of the episode's sixty-six-minute runtime.

This emphasis on the human characters over the zombies continues throughout the first season's six-episode run. What makes the series such an important contribution to the zombie canon, then, is how *The Walking Dead* ups the ante on screen horror by making the characters so well developed, likable, and imperiled. Although the zombies obviously function as catalysts for the show's physical action and apocalyptic story line, the core of *The Walking Dead* addresses the essential concerns of dramatic pathos: the struggles, losses, and emotional traumas experienced by the human protagonists. After Rick awakens from his weeks-long coma, for example, he is understandably bewildered, confused, and shocked by the destruction he finds around him. However, his first emotional breakdown results not from his initial encounter with a desiccated zombie but upon realizing his wife and son are missing and possibly dead. The plot of the next two episodes thus becomes about reuniting Rick with his family first and fighting the walking dead second. All the horror action of the television series is sublimated to its primary focus on the family.

A number of other family relationships contribute fundamentally to the requisite pathos of the series. During the first half of the pilot episode, for instance, Rick encounters Morgan Jones and his son, Duane. In a powerful departure from the comic books, Darabont develops the story of Morgan's zombified wife, whose death and unholy resurrection have visibly traumatized her surviving husband and son. As the episode progresses, the audience realizes the Joneses haven't moved on to the potential safety of Atlanta because Morgan refuses to leave his wife behind. He laments that he cannot kill the creature she has become, even though her continued existence clearly torments both him and his son, who spends his nights sobbing uncontrollably. The scene in which Morgan tries unsuccessfully to shoot his zombie wife with a scoped rifle is particularly moving. He cannot accept the zombie as a soulless monster with no identity or history; Morgan only sees his zombie wife as the human being she once was.

Morgan's struggles with his grief make viewers relate to his humanity, and the episode "Vatos" (1-4), written by Kirkman

himself, introduces and develops additional family relationships with a similar attention to pathos. This installment begins
with Andrea and her younger sister, Amy, fishing together in the
middle of a serene quarry lake. Rather than worrying about
zombies, the two women reminisce about their father, about the
way he had taught them each to fish when they were young girls.
The entire episode centers on similar familial and interpersonal
relationships: Jim wrestles with the guilt of having survived
the initial zombie outbreak at the expense of his wife and children, Daryl risks everything in search of his brother Merle, and
Guillermo belies his tough exterior as the leader of a gang that
cares for the residents of a nursing home. Tragically, the ending
of "Vatos" sees families once again torn apart by the destructive force of the zombie horde, and Amy is brutally killed. The
episode thus comes full circle, but now Andrea is crying over the
bloody body of her young sister.

This fundamental emphasis on humanity makes the television
version of *The Walking Dead* particularly terrifying. However,
the living characters are not the only source of pathos. In addition to being monstrous threats, the zombies are also carefully
depicted in an empathetic light, and this empathy invariably
draws viewers back to the plight of the human characters.
Romero's films deftly use the walking dead to offer scathing
social commentary, but as *Entertainment Weekly* writer Jeff
"Doc" Jensen points out in his article "Dead and Loving It,"
"The zombies of *The Walking Dead* are victims of tragedy, not
metaphors for social satire." Perhaps more than in any other
zombie narrative to date, *The Walking Dead* presents its feckless
monsters as victims, beings that were once human themselves. In
a way, then, zombies are people too, but not in the overly sympathetic manner of pro-zombie narratives such as Marc Price's
low-budget sensation *Colin* (2008), Bruce LaBruce's subversive

Otto; or, Up with Dead People (2008), and the aforementioned novel *Breathers. The Walking Dead* never assigns human emotions and intellectual capacities to its zombies. Instead, the series makes its creatures empathetic because of their *lost* humanity.

Once again, Darabont's vision of the zombie apocalypse draws on the traditions of films such as *Dawn of the Dead* to demonstrate how the walking dead should be pitied as well as feared. From the series' first episode, Rick shows compassion in his dispatching of the zombies, a task he appears to approach in terms of mercy killing. Be it the one-time deputy Leon or the legless female zombie in the park, Rick clearly feels something for these creatures, recognizing them as the human beings they once were. No scene from *The Walking Dead* makes this point more effectively than the one from "Guts" (1-2) in which Rick leads his group in a horrifying dismemberment. Before he begins the grisly task of cutting up a former "walker," Rick pulls out the man's wallet to determine who he once was: Wayne Dunlap. Rick passes the man's driver's license around and says, "He used to be like us. Worrying about bills, the rent, or the Super Bowl. If I ever find my family, I'm going to tell them about Wayne." The tragedy of the zombie infestation goes beyond the physical risks posed by the roaming hordes of monsters. The real horror is that the monsters used to be people—and they represent what might become of the imperiled protagonists.

Of course, the zombies and the humans are fundamentally and unavoidably dissimilar; we pity the former while fearing for the safety of the latter. "Wildfire" (1-5) makes clear additional differences between the living and the dead. After the devastating zombie attack on the refugee camp, Glenn declares that although the dispatched "geeks" should be burned on a pyre, the murdered humans—those from the survivors' group who were killed *before* being transformed into zombies—must be properly buried. In addition, after Jim has been bitten and begins to show signs of infection, Rick prevents Daryl from preemptively euthanizing him: the lawman vehemently points out that even the infected living are still alive, that they remain human beings. Finally, although Andrea keeps others away from her sister's dead body with a cocked pistol, she proves that she too understands the differences between the living and the dead. In perhaps the most touching scene of the entire first season, Andrea waits patiently all night, refusing to defile a corpse she still sees as her human sister; however, once Amy opens her eyes as a zombie, Andrea shoots the monster through the head.

Ultimately, *The Walking Dead* terrifies viewers because its extended narrative format allows fans to develop emotional connections with the characters, and these characters are presented with enough pathos to make audience members fear for their physical well-being. Although viewers pity the tragic monsters, they are more concerned with the safety of the protagonists: viewers feel threatened when Rick and Andrea are in danger, and they feel sadness when Amy and Jim die. One thing that *The Walking Dead* teaches its fan base that can be applied to the entire subgenre is that zombies work best when they are presented *empathetically* but not *sympathetically*. That is, when viewers feel pathos, they experience tragedy, loss, and remorse, emphasizing the reason zombies are so fundamentally terrifying: death isn't the worst thing that can happen to a person; infection and transformation is. Sympathy, on the other hand, asks us to *want* to be zombies. Although this approach may work famously well with mysterious and sexy vampires, such expectations hardly make sense in terms of the shambling, grotesque, and essentially brain-dead zombies. Zombies should be scary, and they can be only when the audience cares about the living heroes.

KYLE WILLIAM BISHOP is a third-generation professor at Southern Utah University, where he teaches courses in American literature, film studies, fantasy literature, and English composition. He has presented and published a variety of articles on cinema and popular culture, covering such subjects as *Metropolis, Night of the Living Dead, Fight Club, Buffy the Vampire Slayer, Dawn of the Dead, The Birds,* and *Zombieland.* Dr. Bishop's first book, *American Zombie Gothic: The Rise and Fall (and Rise) of the Walking Dead in Popular Culture,* is available from McFarland. Online at suu.edu/faculty/bishopk.

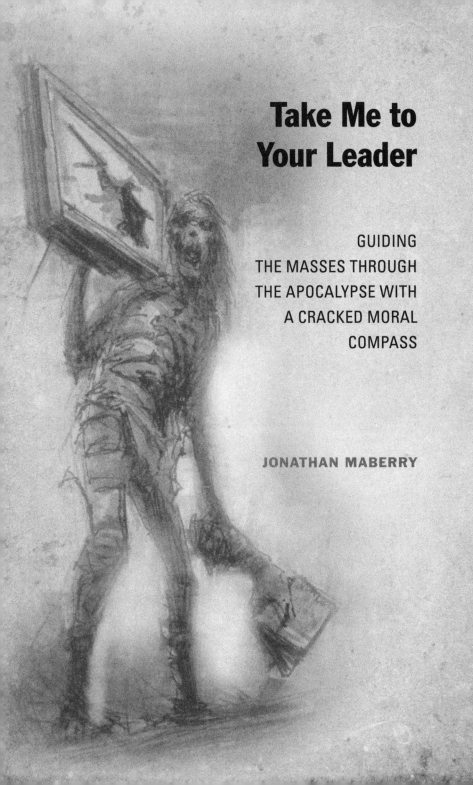

Take Me to Your Leader

GUIDING THE MASSES THROUGH THE APOCALYPSE WITH A CRACKED MORAL COMPASS

JONATHAN MABERRY

sk any random group of people if they think an apocalypse is coming our way, and the majority say yes. A hefty percentage will go so far as to say that it's imminent. Some will be happy to give you a date. Some of them even think that zombies will be players in the global endgame.

So . . . what if they're right? Not necessarily about the zombies—although let's not rule it out—but right about a major event that overwhelmingly alters the world as we know it? It doesn't matter if it's a pandemic, a new Ice Age or other Earth changes, or a solar flare.

If that happens, the first thing we have to do is survive it. Sounds obvious, but it isn't.

Most people are not physically, emotionally, or mentally prepared to survive the apocalypse. Most people have a hard time coping with an interruption of internet access or a dead cell phone, let alone the challenges of finding food and shelter during a total collapse of the infrastructure and in the presence of life-threatening dangers.

In recent years, in the face of hurricanes, earthquakes, and tsunamis, we've seen how quickly order breaks down. You may argue that we've also seen how quickly man rises to his better and braver nature and responds in extraordinary ways to rescue his fellow man. There are countless photos and videos of average citizens risking their lives to pull injured strangers out of collapsed buildings, from raging rivers, and off of flood-encircled rooftops. Sure, that happens; and yay for us. It's proof of the potential in all people to go beyond their comfort zone, step outside their protective social bubble, and do something selfless for another member of the great human tribe. It's an aspect of species survival that we can document and applaud.

However, those documented incidents only exist because there was some kind of structure left to record them: the media, the government, state and local disaster groups, the military. Sure, the government might be reacting slower than normal in an unexpectedly intense event, but they are still there. Survival, in such cases, is often only a matter of waiting until someone official organizes a rescue. The belief in survival is predicated on the knowledge that things will eventually go back to normal. Hell, tourists have returned to New Orleans.

An apocalyptic event does not come with that kind of guarantee.

In fact, it is usually viewed as the kind of event in which no help is coming now, soon, or possibly ever.

The rock band R.E.M. said it: "It's the end of the world as we know it."

In our history we haven't encountered that. Sure, individual cultures have, from Pompeii to the Plains Indians, but overall the human species has not been faced with a situation in which all institutions and all order have been eradicated. That means no cops, no military, no power, no farms, no FEMA. In short, no one is coming.

It's a terrifying thought, even *without* zombies.

SKEWED VIEWS FROM THE END OF DAYS

Philosophers have wrangled about the end of it all since about a minute after language was invented, and fiction authors have taken that ball and run with it in every possible direction, from Mary Shelley's 1827 novel *The Last Man*, in which a deadly plague sweeps the world, right up to *The Walking Dead*, in which Robert Kirkman describes a wasteland where a few humans struggle to survive against hordes of flesh-eating zombies. Between those poles we have hundreds of novels, thousands of short stories, countless comics, and enough TV shows and movies to last even the most diehard couch potato until the actual end of days.

The body of fictional work on the apocalypse is so immense that it has splintered to produce many subgenres and even sub-subgenres, ranging from utterly bleak tales of the ultimate failure of everything—society, morals, courage, hope—to tales that chronicle an optimistic view of new life rising from the ashes of the old world. There are no elements that unite all of them, of course, except perhaps that apocalyptic tales generally stand as metaphors for things we fear in our as-yet-undestroyed world; however, the most common thread is the dim view they take of civilization.

The view most frequently espoused by writers is that civilization as we know it would not survive an apocalypse, even if people did. It's not that we *couldn't* survive, but the cynical—and overwhelmingly common—view is that we won't.

Here's the logic for why the odds aren't in our favor in a global disaster: We have become fatally soft, weakened by the technology that has allowed us to conquer the rest of the planet. The weakness comes from being continually resource-rich in our daily lives. We have clothing, multiple forms of transportation, medicine, readily available food sources, deliveries of goods, affordable repairs or replaceable parts, and access to virtually endless information via cell phones and internet. When we feel helpless or threatened, we know that there are various levels of protection, from security guards in our shopping malls to cops to the military. When we are confused, we have all manner of leaders to tell us what to do and how to think. The fact that we are surrounded by structure encourages us to believe in its effectiveness and permanence.

If the system fails, we are no longer conditioned to react quickly and appropriately; nor are we conditioned to react on our own. Generally speaking, the average person in a post-industrial society is not skilled in repairs, combat, farming, emergency medicine, outdoor survival, general mechanics, or other useful trades.

Our weakness is exacerbated by our trust that the system will always reset itself. Once the system fails and we become convinced of its failure, that's when we stop being who we are. Where once we were empowered by being members of complex and resource-rich societies, we suddenly become individually weaker, which in turn weakens the species. We drop way lower on the food chain, and we become less prepared for long-term survival than, say, your cat, Mr. Snuffles.

Panic can come into play at a couple of points here, and with different degrees of intensity. When a disaster happens, there is the immediate reactive panic, the kind you get when you live in a Kansas trailer home and you look out the window and see a category-five tornado cutting across the parking lot toward you.

Then there's the blind "What the hell is happening?" panic you get when people from the East Coast experience their first West Coast earthquake. Ideally in an elevator.

There's also the panic associated with the group dynamic, the mob-hysteria mentality that can transform Joe Average into a store-window-smashing, TV-set-grabbing rioter if the moment is right.

In the kind if apocalypse we're describing, all of those come into play. Sudden shock, a shortage of the kind of information that can help you get your bearings, and shared fear.

Now add zombies to the mix.

THIS IS HOW WE FALL

In the early stages of a zombie apocalypse, there will be some protection as people band together in social subgroups to confront the situation, such as "the people in our office building versus the zombies." Then, as the danger mounts and resources diminish, it becomes "the people on our floor, and so sorry about everyone on the other floors." Then it's "the people in our department," "in our office," "in this room," "in this stairwell," and finally, "me." Weakness and uncertainty breed fear and panic. Ask anyone from a psychologist to a lifeguard—panic gets you killed.

In many apocalyptic stories, as the structure, services, resources, and technology of civilization fail, so do man's higher ideals. Charity, mercy, compassion, benevolence, tolerance, generosity, patience, and kindness are killed off somewhere around the end of the first act, often never to be seen again. And if these qualities do resurface, they do so in so rare and fragile a way as to suggest ultimate hopelessness even in a hopeful ending.

Good examples of this can be found in the endings of the first three of George Romero's Living Dead films. At the end of *Night of the Living Dead* (1968), none of the people who have struggled all night—against the hordes of zombies and against each other—survive. Even the stalwart Ben is gunned down in the final reel. In *Dawn of the Dead* (1978), after a new paradise is found by refugees fleeing the zombie holocaust, things go south and almost everybody dies. And in *Day of the Dead*

(1985), there is a retread of this, where bickering and infighting among surviving humans leads to a zombie chowdown.

So now we're down to it. Zombies are eating people and no one is coming to help. People have scattered and there are fewer and fewer of them. The more people panic, the more bad choices they make; the more bad choices they make, the easier it is for everyone to become totally self-centered savages.

In a zombie apocalypse, this is the path to savagery. It's the one thing that the idealists and the cynics agree upon.

That's how we fall.

The question is really about how we get up again. Or if we do.

In the cynical view, we don't. And even in those rare cases when the good guys escape in the final reel, we're left with a pessimistic view of what's next. The endings only *seem* to be happy. In Romero's *Dawn of the Dead*, everyone dies except for two adults, one of whom is pregnant. Happy ending? Really? Try to pull a new race of humans out of a gene pool that shallow. Within a few decades—providing they don't find other people, which is shown to be unlikely—the final generation of mankind would be inbred half-wits. In *Day of the Dead*, two men and a woman escape in a helicopter to what appears to be an island paradise. Again we have survivors—and we did come to root for these folks—but there is no potential for ultimate species survival. In Zack Snyder's re-imagining of *Dawn of the Dead* (2004), we have two men and two women escaping by boat— but if you sit through the end credits you see that this ending isn't exactly happy either. We don't *know* that they all die, but a Vegas odds-maker would happily take your money if you wanted to bet on their survival.

This is something common to postapocalyptic stories. It isn't that there are no people of intelligence, resourcefulness, and good will in the tales; it's just that not enough of them survive.

Even if a group of survivors bands together, the trend in apocalyptic storytelling is to have their new social structure disintegrate into infighting, which opens the door, metaphorically and literally, to a renewed attack by the living dead.

The cynics tell us that we're doomed, no matter how hard we try.

However, there is another view, and it's one that Robert Kirkman has been exploring in *The Walking Dead*.

Kirkman builds on the same tropes as Romero and his many followers: the worldwide zombie plague has crashed humanity, the infrastructure is gone, the survivors are few and scattered, and there is brutal infighting among those who are left. What Kirkman does, however, is explore the one element that will very likely be the thing that separates us from extinction and gives us the chance to take back the world.

In short, a leader.

A leader with balls, guns, brains, and a mission.

Sanity? Not really a job requirement.

ALWAYS LOOK ON THE BRIGHT SIDE OF LIFE

Despite the fact that the *Walking Dead* comic book is one of the bleakest, most downbeat and nihilistic stories ever told, even in a genre known for those qualities, Kirkman manages to sew a thread of hope through the tale. This doesn't mean that he went soft on us when he created *The Walking Dead*; far, far from it. There are plenty of bad guys, dumb guys, backstabbing guys, cannibal guys, and every other kind of human predator guy. Of course there are. There would be, just as there are right now. Human corruption and evil are not specific to the zombie apocalypse. We've pretty much had those since Cain introduced Abel to Mr. Blunt Instrument.

However, Kirkman approaches the issue of survival with a certain clarity of vision that requires neither opaque black shades nor rose-colored glasses. He's always looking at both the forest and the trees.

Kirkman's hero, Rick Grimes, is no Mad Max. He's not a postapocalyptic action hero who always has a plan. He's not the brilliant scientist-hero of the recent film adaptation of Richard Matheson's *I Am Legend* (2007). Rick is none of those things, and probably the last word he would be likely to use to describe himself is "hero."

The Walking Dead, both the comic book and the TV series, isn't about the rise of a hero or the hero's journey, not in the pop culture sense of the word "hero." The series is not, in fact, about heroes at all. It's about someone discovering within himself a sense of purpose that is every bit as infectious as the disease that made the dead rise. For Rick, it's all about saving those he loves. It's a focused mission, but if others want to come along for the ride and share in the benefits, then that's okay with Rick.

And within that mission is the potential for it to evolve and grow. In a sense, Rick starts off in the same place as the troubled masses we discussed in the previous section. He has been reduced to a lone frightened and weakened person. He is a victim and appears to be without resources.

Rick is a cop, a husband, a dad. And he possesses one crucial quality: optimism. His optimism is very badly dented, and the warranty is about to run out, but he still has it. And I'll argue that this, too, is natural to our species. It explains our survival in a world of terrible natural predators, and it offers a clue as to why we are now at the top of the food chain. Rick believes that there has to be an end to struggle, a place of safety, somewhere he can take his family and stop running. And when other characters follow him, it's because they've caught the optimism infection. Hope, however small a thing, is a shining light in dark times.

What separates Rick from other characters in the story is that he goes from victim to father/husband/protector, to group leader, to a new kind of warlord.

Here's the short version of how that plays out.

Kirkman introduces Rick as a small-town lawman who gets shot at a simple roadblock. He gets the bad guys, but the bad guys get him too. Roll forward, and Rick wakes up in a hospital, alone, helpless, vulnerable.

Except . . . in the comic, Rick demonstrates two key qualities early on, and they're fueled by a third. His immediate reaction is that of self-preservation, which requires information and action. Rick gets out of his hospital bed and goes looking for answers. He discovers that everyone is dead, but the dead aren't quite as dead as they should be. Rick gets the hell out of there. So far he's doing what anyone would do, which means he's still a helpless individual and not yet a leader.

The second thing Rick does is try to reconnect with his "tribe": he goes home. We are comforted and strengthened by familiar people and places. Within a family group (or, by extension, a team, club, clan, etc.), we feel empowered. At the outset, as Rick flees the hospital, he may be seeking safety by returning home, but with each moment that he survives, his need changes from immediate personal security to a desire to protect his family. This is tribalism at its grandest: the alpha attempting to gather his scattered pack and defend them with the shared power of unity. Very basic stuff, but very important. This is also a defining characteristic of Rick's. It is the mission that will save him, and might help him eventually save the world.

Unfortunately for Rick, his wife Lori and their son Carl are not at home. At first Rick despairs, thinking that they've been killed along with everyone else. But here we have a moment where intellect asserts itself over simple human instinct, because Rick examines the house and sees that there are family pictures missing. This is evidence that Rick, both as a father and as a cop, observes and analyzes. He realizes that only Lori would bother to take those photos with her, since they're of no value to anyone else during this crisis. Therefore, Lori might still be alive. Rick's mission is now driven by the possibility of finding and saving his family.

This leads him to do the third thing that firmly sets him on the path to leadership: he goes to his old police station, puts on his uniform, and gathers up his weapons. Rick doesn't need to wear the badge or the Smokey the Bear hat, but the uniform provides him with a kind of armor; it transforms him from survivor to knight. He will henceforth act upon his sense of duty. Not always well, and not always in the way that truly serves the public good, but that sense of duty is the moral compass that will drive him. It gives purpose to his survival. Ultimately it will become Rick's defining characteristic, as throughout the series the other characters (not all, but most) defer to him because he has claimed his personal authority while most of the others have not.

During this process, Rick also meets other survivors, and from them he learns about the plague and the fall of humanity. We can view these characters as advisors to the leader, providing necessary information but not participating in the executive decisions Rick needs to make. At this point, Rick is focused on his family, and although he is compassionate about the experiences and needs of the others he meets, their survival is not yet his mission. In effect, he is trying to reclaim leadership of his own tribe and is not willing or able to lead a new tribe.

That will change.

I FOUGHT THE LAW AND THE LAW WON

Laws do not create or sustain themselves. They are decisions made, enacted, and enforced by groups of people, ostensibly for the common good. When a society collapses, it can be argued that the laws of that society are no longer in force unless a significant number of the survivors agree that those laws still govern them. In an apocalyptic scenario, survival is based more upon needs as defined by a pack mentality. The strongest lead; everyone else follows.

In *The Walking Dead*, Rick reintroduces the element of law into the zombie apocalypse. At first he is a tribe of one, and the laws he introduces are his own. This is underscored nicely in the second episode of the TV show, when Rick has a run-in with Earle, a violent and antisocial redneck who embodies all that was wrong with the old world: racism, intolerance, indifference to suffering, and a love of violence for its own sake. Rick witnesses Earle beating a black man for no other apparent reason than skin color. The attack is not only cruel, but it puts Rick's tribe of one at risk by drawing the attention of zombies. So Rick kicks the crap out of Earle, handcuffs him, and when the redneck demands to know who he is, Rick replies with what will become the manifesto for the tribe of one: "I'm a man looking for his wife and son. Anybody gets in the way of that's gonna lose."

There it is. The first law of the postapocalyptic world, articulated by a man who has embraced his power and is determined to use every bit of it to accomplish his mission.

As Rick moves forward with that mission, he picks up other people. At times he allows them to join him in shared protection, though he always makes it clear that he prioritizes his family over everyone else. No exceptions.

Once Rick finds his wife and reestablishes his personal tribe, the door is opened for that tribe to expand. Lori and Carl are part of another tribe of survivors, and Rick's friend and fellow cop Shane is their de facto leader. Shane shares some qualities with Rick—physical strength, police training, knowledge of weapons, some tactical skills—but he does not have the absolute drive that Rick has.

It's not clear whether Shane would have made as good a leader as Rick. Shane is more timid, less likely to take risks. It's possible he is even more sane than Rick. He might have been able to keep more of the survivors alive . . . or his timidity and indecision might have resulted in a gradual and fatal depletion of resources. That tantalizing question is never explored, because Shane dies early on in the comic book series. For better or worse, that leaves Rick as the most capable leader.

FOLLOW THE LEADER

As the story progresses, Rick makes a lot of crucial decisions about survival, including some really bad ones. And because of his decisions, people sometimes die. If we Monday morning quarterback that, we can call good and bad plays; but the apocalypse is ongoing, and it's hard to see the big picture beyond what needs to happen right now to stay alive.

Often this is a case of Rick doing what he feels is best for his family and the other survivors following along. Sometimes his decisions are in opposition to those of the group at large, but at no point does Rick yield command of his personal tribe. It's clear to the other characters that he is willing to leave them behind if he has to.

This is hardly a rallying cry, but it has that effect. Because Rick seemingly cannot be deterred, even after emotional loss and frequent physical injuries—at one point the Governor, a far more corrupt leader of a different tribe, cuts Rick's hand off—Rick keeps going. His enemies fall around him, even if not always by his hand. Rick walks over mountains of the dead, including some who were his friends, in order to keep his tribe alive. His very survival confers upon him a façade of invulnerability. It makes him a symbol, and people follow symbols. (That's one of the reasons the Pope wears such a funny hat.)

The longer Rick survives, the more he shifts from a desperate man fighting to live into a legendary leader who symbolizes the struggle of all humanity through the end times. This process grants him strength while at the same time fracturing him emotionally and psychologically. Kirkman gives us glimpses of Rick's inner turmoil and his desperate self-awareness by allowing us to eavesdrop on private conversations between Rick and other characters, and later by showing Rick's psychotic phone conversations with his dead wife. These glimpses—scattered lightly throughout the comic book series—deepen our respect for Rick because we see the terrible cost of his continuing mission. Nevertheless, he keeps moving, and over time the familiarity with the other survivors nudges Rick in the direction of including them in his own extended tribe.

Kirkman does not, however, paint Rick as a spotless hero. Like many leaders fighting for survival against virtually impossible odds, Rick is still a law unto himself, the Ten Commandments and the Constitution be damned. There is the Law of Rick and Rick's Tribe, and Kirkman shows how unpleasant it is to get between the man and those he loves.

THE WARLORD AND THE WALKING DEAD

We all know that recording history is a sanitizing process. We edit out the details we don't like. We may celebrate our soldiers, but few citizens want to see with unfiltered clarity what those soldiers have to do to win a battle. And people don't want to be confronted with the fact that the Founding Fathers could not agree on a resolution to abolish slavery, or that Washington owned slaves, or, hell, that the White House was built by slave labor. We don't focus on the blood-and-guts particulars of our nation's most significant battles. We know that the North won the Battle of Gettysburg, but history books don't include raw descriptions of men wrestling in the mud, biting fingers, or gouging out eyes with their thumbs. Even now we talk about "settling the West," and not about the comprehensive germ warfare we carried out against Native Americans by giving them blankets known to be infested with smallpox and chicken pox. What matters to the modern, civilized person is that we are currently civilized and moral.

Except that we're not. We are at war, and war is not fought nicely. We torture and we kill, we carpet-bomb, and sometimes innocent civilians die in order for a battle to be won or a significant enemy defeated.

Those decisions are made, for good or ill, by leaders.

Leaders such as Rick Grimes. His story shows us how leaders emerge, how they are forged, how they are shaped, and how they are burned into the pages of history.

By issue eighty-four of *The Walking Dead*, the conclusion to the epic "No Way Out" story arc, Rick has reached a watershed moment. The Alexandria Safe-Zone has been saved after the zombies have breached the walls and flooded the town, but only through the collective action of the strongest of the survivors. After suffering incredible loss—including the loss of Jessie, with whom he had become romantically involved, and the potentially fatal wounding of Carl—Rick realizes how he and the remaining survivors might move forward, not only to rebuild their defenses, but to expand the settlement. He finally accepts that he is, in fact, the leader. This is the point where the mentality of prey/survivor is burned away, leaving behind a new kind of creature: a predator, perhaps even a conqueror. Someone who has looked out across the world and decided that it needs to be conquered. It is a moment Rick shares with Alexander the Great, Napoleon, and Suleiman the Magnificent.

Rick decides to take back the world. Or, looked at another way, Rick decides to *conquer* the world.

He finally reaches that crucial moment, as certainly our earliest leaders did, when he realizes that there is no way to protect his nomadic and dwindling tribe if that tribe is always running. They can't simply turn and make a stand, though, because the enemy he fights will never stop and will never recognize a boundary. Zombies don't acknowledge threats. So Rick decides to go on the offensive. He wants his tribe to stop fleeing and become an invading horde.

We can even see how he'll do it: With ruthlessness and hard choices. Without sentimentality. With an absolute disdain for his enemies. Sure, there are six billion zombies and a pitiful few humans. We know that. But Rick has seen firsthand that, one on one, zombies are no match for a human with basic combat skills, and by this point all of the survivors have that. Rick himself has killed hundreds of the undead by now. Some of his people have killed as many or more.

When Rick decides to fight back, we see him come into his own as the leader. He has embraced that role completely, with a will, and with ferocity.

This is Rick the Leader, finally and totally. Rick has earned his role as leader by virtue of never wavering from his mission, never allowing even the cruelest circumstance to stop him. He has become the living embodiment of the big picture, of the big dream of a new and better world.

Will Rick the Leader be a shining example of heroic purity? Not a chance. He's damaged goods.

In the comics, Kirkman has done a masterful job of chronicling the mental, physical, and emotional erosion of someone who is forced to make constant hard (and sometimes clearly bad) choices. It's a process of erosion that, for most people, does lasting harm. It gradually replaces healthy flesh with scar tissue, and there is often a point where disfiguring scars are all that seem to remain, leaving behind someone who has lost touch with his or her basic humanity. Kirkman gives us two variations on this theme with the brutal and twisted Governor and Alexander Davidson, the disgraced founder of the Alexandria Safe-Zone—the latter of whom started out with good intentions and fell from grace along the way. Both were men whose path to leadership destroyed too much of their essential humanity.

Could this happen to Rick? If he keeps making hard choices, will he become too thoroughly hardened himself? Similarly, if Rick continues to make bad choices—such as injuring, killing, or allowing the killing of members of his extended tribe in order to promote their security—will he become a monster like the Governor?

I don't think so. Although Rick is capable of being damaged, he isn't capable of being corrupted. Victims of his bad decisions might disagree (those who survive those decisions, anyway), but the story of The Walking Dead is the story of Rick Grimes, and Kirkman has not been chronicling a descent into corruption and evil. Even at its darkest and most grim, there is a thread of optimism and idealism sewn through the fabric of each comic and each episode of the TV show. All along, Rick has struggled to do what's right and has been aware of his actions when he's done wrong. His increasing psychosis—and the degree to which he's aware of it—demonstrates his struggle against personal mental and moral disintegration. At the worst, Rick may become so thoroughly damaged that he might not be a fit member for the new society he creates. He may die at the gates of whatever new paradise rises from the ashes of the old world. But it's just as likely that he will find his mental and emotional footing and heal stronger in the places where he was broken.

When reading *The Walking Dead*, one can easily peer into the future, to a time when the tribes of survivors manage to take back the world from the living dead. We can imagine how future generations will describe Rick. They will probably overlook his many flaws and exaggerate his virtues. Although Rick is not a hero, and *The Walking Dead* is not a story about heroes, history would nevertheless transform Rick from man into hero. The bad things he did would be either excused, justified, or simply edited out of most versions of his tale. Remember how most high school history books don't mention that the White House was built by slave labor? So, yeah, the history of the community he's working to found would paint Rick as a heroic leader. That's what history does.

The Rick of the first eighty-three issues of the comic book would be appalled by this propaganda. The Rick of issue eighty-four and beyond would probably sneer at it and hate it—but he would understand. His understanding would spring from the knowledge that, without leaders, we could not survive so vast a catastrophe. Without leaders, society could not reform and rebuild—at least not a new version of the old world. More likely, life would become something that we, in a preapocalyptic world, can't truly imagine. Whatever emerges, though, will only be created through leadership. Without leaders, laws and rules of behavior would not become part of our culture, and even the most libertarian among us acknowledge that some rules are necessary.

At this writing, I don't know where Kirkman will go with Rick's new vision—the revelation about community he gained after the epic battle to save the Alexandria Safe-Zone that concluded the "No Way Out" story arc. I'd been expecting a dramatic change of this kind, however, and I'm glad that Kirkman respected the process of history enough not to have played this card earlier. I fully expect that Rick the Leader will continue to make mistakes, and continue to make hard choices, even if some of those choices prove to be the wrong ones. I expect him to find more cracks in his sanity. After all, we have never really required our leaders to be totally sane.

Kirkman has a lot of story he can tell. *The Walking Dead* began as an apocalyptic tale that showed us the Fall; then it moved into a postapocalyptic tale as Rick and his tribe fought for survival on a day-to-day basis in a world stolen from them by the living dead. Now it seems that Kirkman is moving into a new direction. Will Rick lead his tribe from the dark ruins of the zombie wasteland up into the light to create a utopia (or at least a new version of civilized society), or will a dystopia be built on the bones of the old world?

Despite all the pain and suffering, hard and bad choices, if anyone is going to guide the tribe of humanity out of the darkness, it will be Rick Grimes, or someone very much like him: a leader with at least one unbroken thread of idealism holding together the pieces of a broken heart.

JONATHAN MABERRY is a *New York Times* bestselling and multiple Bram Stoker Award-winning author, magazine feature writer, playwright, content creator, and writing teacher/lecturer. His novels include action thrillers (*Patient Zero*); teen zombie thrillers (*Rot & Ruin*); supernatural thrillers (*Ghost Road Blues*); movie tie-ins (*The Wolfman*); and horror (*Dead of Night*). His nonfiction books include *Vampire Universe*, *The Cryptopedia*, *They Bite!* (with David F. Kramer), *Zombie CSU: The Forensics of the Living Dead*, and *Wanted Undead or Alive*. His work for Marvel includes *Captain America: Hail Hydra*, *Black Panther*, *Doomwar*, and *Marvel Zombies Return*. Jonathan is a frequent guest of honor or keynote speaker at writers' and genre conferences. Online at jonathanmaberry.com or follow him on Twitter @jonathanmaberry.

Four-Color Zombies

THE WALKING DEAD IN
COMICS HISTORY

ARNOLD T. BLUMBERG

n the midst of a massive surge of zombie-themed entertainment, *The Walking Dead* has been held up not only as an example of compelling comic book storytelling but as a flag bearer for the medium. The series' allegorical exploration of the human condition and the success of its television adaptation have drawn many people into their local comic shops for *Walking Dead* collections. For students of comics history, there is a certain delicious irony in the fact that a raw, gory, terrifying saga centered around a world plagued by the living dead has become an Eisner Award–winning success—and one of the best comics published today. Decades ago, the title would have been held up as evidence in a Senate subcommittee meeting. Copies would have been burned for a calculated photo op while pundits pontificated about the ways the publication was rotting the brains of our nation's youth. In those days, *The Walking Dead* would never have survived, but, paradoxically, without the anti-horror comics hysteria of the forties and fifties, this series might never have come into existence at all.

Soulless, unthinking, hungry monsters. Creatures from the depths of hell were marching en masse to consume the citizens of this great nation and destroy everything we knew and loved. Armed only with his intellect and the weapons of his trade, one man was determined to stand before this horde of horrors and defend his home from their slavering, animalistic wrath. Yes,

Senator Joseph McCarthy would stop the Communists from taking over the United States if it was the last thing he would ever do.

America emerged from the shadow of World War II and exchanged the certainty of Axis evil for the more insidious threat of Communist infiltration. The United States of the early 1950s was a country of contradictions, proud and prosperous, with suburban temples to the perfection of family life sprouting up all over, but also plagued by lurking terrors. Beneath the freshly mown lawns hid atomic bomb shelters and deep-seated doubts. There were reports of soldiers returning from the Korean War with radically changed personalities and vacant stares, behaving as if they were mere puppets subjugated to the controlling will of an evil master. Their behavior did, in fact, resemble that of— oh, what is that word?

But the "brainwashing" Reds, immortalized in Richard Condon's incendiary 1959 tale of assassination and Communist dupes, *The Manchurian Candidate*, were just one threat contributing to an ever-widening sense of instability felt by every American. Even as McCarthy's politically motivated efforts to weed out Communists in our midst waned in the early fifties, a fellow senator named Estes Kefauver shifted the focus away from the more nebulous threat of Communists and onto the slightly more concrete menace of youth crime—and comic books. The enemies were no longer faceless spies and ideologues from another country; they were publishing entrepreneurs right here at home, and they were transforming our children into a horde of mindless, marauding monsters known as "juvenile delinquents."

This was the comic book scare of the 1950s, "the ten-cent plague," the nationwide censorship craze that almost wiped a literary art form out of existence. The comics industry had thrived after its initial burst of creative and financial success in the

1930s, with superheroes riding a patriotic wave through World War II as emblems of American might. In the postwar world, comics struggled to find a new focus as the superhero genre waned. Publishers found themselves pushing the bounds of taste with increasingly shocking tales of crime, sex, and horror.

While this material was viewed by some as a threat in itself, it actually offered up a way for Americans to confront their postwar fears and understand them. As always, the era's pop culture provided a potential catharsis through music, in television and movies, and in comic book pages, as a new, distinctive youth culture strained against the bonds of tradition and adult supervision, rebelling against all things "square." This rebellion defined itself with the help of those lurid comic book tales of criminal depravity, wild romantic abandon, and grotesque nightmares. Although there were many publishers gleefully serving up the material, the indisputable king of the graveyard was William M. Gaines, publisher of EC Comics.

While it's true that the industry's most infamous purveyor of corpse-ridden comics was pushing boundaries and demonstrating the medium's potential through tales about racism ("In Gratitude . . ."; *Shock SuspenStories* 11, October–November 1953) and religion ("He Walked Among Us"; *Weird Science* 13, May–June 1952), EC's critics weren't entirely wrong when they claimed the company's comics were going too far for younger readers. Defensive comic fans who grew up with the fan-generated party line are often quick to defend EC, but anyone who reads just a few pages of its usual horror fare will find plenty of material inappropriate for young kids in any era. EC reveled in presenting readers with an endless assortment of moldering undead, flesh dripping from exposed bone as they clawed their way out of the earth and sought the living.

There was at least the notion that most of this cadaverous activity had a reason. The narrative use of the zombie as the embodiment of vengeance had already been explored many times, especially in early zombie-themed movies—several starring Boris Karloff (and one of them even titled *The Walking Dead*). The zombie as a pop culture icon originated in film, and comics certainly took their cues from that medium. EC was one of several publishers that cemented this interpretation of the zombie and gave all their devoted "kiddies" countless ghouls and grotesques to terrify them as they turned the pages and then settled in for a sleepless night. But while many of the zombies that trudged through EC's pages were meting out some form of unholy justice—revenge for a wrongful death or punishment for wicked behavior—there were ghouls that returned just for the buffet of living flesh. Regardless of their motives, the zombies and their creature cousins led EC to the epicenter of a cultural crisis.

There had been attempts in the 1940s to demonize comics, part of an almost inevitable cultural backlash after the medium had achieved a level of popularity sufficient to draw the attention of those for whom moral outrage was a way of life. However, the hysteria didn't reach fever pitch until the 1950s, when it drew its two most noteworthy champions. Senator Kefauver's work in investigating interstate commerce garnered him a great deal of media coverage as he clashed with the colorful characters of organized crime. Child psychologist Dr. Fredric Wertham was a well-known comics-hating pundit who had already built his reputation with articles about the evils of the art form. Both men found a common cause in comics and took to a national stage to tell the American citizens about the danger in their midst.

Wertham's book on the comic book "crisis," *Seduction of the Innocent*, was previewed in the pages of *Ladies' Home Journal* in November 1953 and hit bookshelves in early 1954. Trading torches and pitchforks for television broadcasts and endless op-eds, the censorship brigade was now armed to hunt down what they thought were the real monsters in the world—comic book publishers, the creators of all those juvenile delinquents. Kefauver and Wertham may have been unlikely allies, but the Baptist senator from Tennessee and the German-Jewish expatriate were about to make pop culture history and write themselves into the nightmares of dedicated comic enthusiasts for decades to come.

It all came down to two days in April 1954. Kefauver's subcommittee held hearings on the comics industry and its links with juvenile delinquency. The hearings were run by another of Kefauver's lesser partners in the crusade, Senator Robert C. Hendrickson from New Jersey. Wertham and a few others testified, offering questionable but seemingly definitive statements about the threat posed by these publications, but the man who drove the final nail in the coffin for this era of horror comics was William M. Gaines himself.

Allegedly popping prescribed Dexedrine tablets before taking the stand, Gaines first offered a coherent statement defending comics as an art form and then descended into incoherence as he crashed from the drugs and folded under questioning. At one point he claimed to be the first publisher of a horror comic, with a book he released in January 1950. This was far from accurate, as horror had already been well represented in comics during the 1940s; even Carl Barks, one of the most celebrated storytellers for children in pop culture history, had introduced Donald Duck to Bombie the Zombie in *Four Color* 238 in August 1949. His foggy history aside, Gaines' testimony lost coherence entirely as examples of EC comics were brought out by the subcommittee for Gaines to defend.

As recorded for posterity in the actual transcripts and retold in books such as David Hajdu's *The Ten-Cent Plague: The Great Comic-Book Scare and How It Changed America* (2008), the man who once told prospective writers in a *Writer's Digest* ad that EC loves "walking corpse stories . . . we'll accept an occasional zombie or mummy" was forced to acknowledge to the subcommittee, the attending press and guests, and countless viewers watching on television at home that he thought a recent EC cover depicting a beheaded woman was in fact tasteful because it cut the image off before showing any of the blood dripping from her neck. Any comics publishers watching at home knew at once that the battle was lost.

In a last desperate attempt to save the comics industry as he knew it, Gaines rallied comic publishers together to self-regulate and stave off government intervention. The appeal was a success, but when the Comics Magazine Association of America (CMAA) was incorporated on September 7, 1954, with Archie Comics' John Goldwater as its charter president, the code it intended to implement to save the industry outlawed everything that had made EC a sales leader. By the time the Comic Book Code was enacted on October 27, 1954, Gaines had already publicly admitted defeat. The CMAA had no legal authority, but many stores would carry only comic books branded with its Comics Code Authority (CCA) seal of approval.

It's interesting to consider that *The Walking Dead* would have been impossible to publish under the auspices of the code. In fact, the series bears as its title the very phrase with which its central creatures were outlawed by the code:

Scenes dealing with, or instruments associated with *walking dead*, torture, vampires and vampirism, ghouls, cannibalism and werewolfism are prohibited. [emphasis added]

The Walking Dead also indulges in many other aspects of storytelling proscribed by the code. As just one example, the infamous story arc in which Michonne is repeatedly tortured and raped by the perverted Governor would have easily violated a number of specific code clauses, including:

> Scenes of excessive violence shall be prohibited. Scenes of brutal torture, excessive and unnecessary knife and gun play, physical agony, gory and gruesome crime shall be eliminated [. . .]

> All scenes of horror, excessive bloodshed, gory or gruesome crimes, depravity, lust, sadism, masochism shall not be permitted [. . .]

> All lurid, unsavory, gruesome illustrations shall be eliminated.

In addition to the many longer-term effects of the code on comic book creation, the short-term result was the virtual annihilation of the horror comic genre and the end of EC's industry dominance. Only one of EC's titles went on to any success at all, but what a success it was. Its humor comic, *Mad*, became a cultural phenomenon all its own when Gaines sidestepped the code by shifting it from comic book to magazine format; this strategy would come into play again in the history of horror comics a few years later. As for the censors, their interest soon turned to another youth movement as Elvis shook his hips on television and introduced the adult world to the shocking hedonism of rock and roll.

Monsters continued to rear their sanitized heads in comics from time to time after the establishment of the code, but usually in a superhero adventure or science-fiction context, as alien beings from far-flung worlds or other dimensions. The few remaining horror comics that tried to provide censored chills did so with diminishing returns. Zombies, however, were driven from the medium as the code built its walls and placed sentries at the gates to ward off any further infiltration by the walking dead. But, as everyone knows, zombies can only be temporarily thwarted, not defeated.

In 1958, Warren Publishing launched a magazine-format tribute to horror cinema, *Famous Monsters of Filmland*, under the guidance of Forrest J. Ackerman. The magazine helped to rally horror fans with its combination of cheeky humor and reverential coverage of movies both classic and contemporary, but what publisher James Warren really wanted to do was print the best horror comics anyone had ever seen. There was surely no way to do that in the comics industry of the time, so he decided to follow the same route that Gaines had used to save *Mad*. Warren was about to bring the zombies and all their ghoulish, bloodthirsty friends back to comic pages, but the pages were bigger than ever before and the talent gathered to tell their tales would be incomparable—including many former EC creators!

Creepy launched in 1964. *Eerie* followed a year later. As detailed in David A. Roach and Jon B. Cooke's *The Warren Companion* (2001), Warren's goal was to provide high-quality horror story-telling without the "bad taste" issues that had plagued EC and without simply imitating the doomed comics publisher. A combination of writers and illustrators who had once made EC the pinnacle of the comics market and newcomers who would one day be lauded as stars in their own right—such as Neal Adams, Gray Morrow, and Bernie Wrightson—offered tales that were terrifying, challenging, and filled with the sort of violence and sexuality that would never have passed muster with the code.

While Warren gave horror fans a new source of comics mayhem and proved to publishers and creators that there were ways around the code, other changes in the traditional comics industry were already suggesting that the code's hegemony would be short-lived. In 1961, Marvel Comics launched its new line of superhero titles, capturing the imagination of college-age readers with a more realistic depiction (for the time) of its lead heroes. Other publishers followed suit, but the change in tone wasn't occurring in the comics world alone—the entire culture was growing up. This maturation in attitudes about sex, race, and many other topics was reflected in music, movies, and literature. As always, comics were not so much leading the way as mirroring what was going on around them. Readers no longer wanted pure escapism; they wanted their comics to tackle more serious issues. So comic book publishers delivered, or delivered as best they could.

The code still limited what the mainstream companies could offer readers, but the 1960s and early 1970s saw the emergence of a creative movement that blended the comics medium with the underground youth scene, mixing social commentary with explicit sexuality, drug use, and violence. Later labeled "undergrounds" or "comix," these small-press and self-published comic books created controversial new stars such as Robert Crumb and Gilbert Shelton while establishing new means of production and distribution, which were necessary to get the books into the hands of those readers who wanted things expressly outlawed by the Comic Book Code. Over-the-top horror titles such as *Bogeyman* (1969), *Skull Comics* (1970), *Insect Fear* (1970), and yes, *Two-Fisted Zombies* (1973) couldn't be found on a spinner rack at the local newsstand or even ordered through the major distribution houses. They could, however, be found at head shops, whose proprietors got them from alternative distributors along with their underground newspapers.

As the 1960s shuddered to a close, the mainstream comics world struggled to prove its relevance to more mature readers. This was no easy feat, since the code still restricted much of the story content that would be necessary if a comic book hero were to, say, confront the drug crisis among the nation's youth. It didn't matter that the work was intended to make an anti-drug statement; the very depiction of drug addiction was verboten. This would lead to a historic first, as Marvel's Stan Lee defied the code and published issues of *The Amazing Spider-Man* (96–98, May–July 1971) without the Comics Code Authority seal in order to tell kids about the evils of LSD. Somewhere the ghouls were grinning; the CCA, recognizing that the code had fallen behind the times, and perhaps acknowledging the pressure from a consumer base that appreciated the many options being offered by artists working with underground publishers, was about to crack the crypt door open just a bit.

In 1971, a new version of the code was enacted. Much of the language remained the same, but the CCA loosened some of the more stringent requirements, enabling comics creators working with the mainstream publishers to tell more socially aware stories. If their tales could not be as frank as the material that had already been in circulation via the undergrounds, they were at least a step in the right direction. There was, however, one specific species of creature that still didn't make the CCA's cut:

Scenes dealing with, or instruments associated with walking dead, or torture, shall not be used. Vampires, ghouls and werewolves shall be permitted to be used when handled in the classic tradition such as Frankenstein, Dracula, and other high caliber literary works written by Edgar Allen [*sic*] Poe, Saki, Conan Doyle and other respected authors whose works are read in schools around the world.

Marvel didn't wait long to take advantage of the looser rules, and the result was a massive boom in series built around modern interpretations of classic horror characters. This wasn't the first time the company had mined that vein, since the Marvel superheroes that helped to reawaken the industry—Spider-Man, the Thing of the Fantastic Four, the X-Men—were themselves science-fiction variations on the monsters that Lee and cohorts Jack Kirby and Steve Ditko had employed during their own run of horror comics in the 1950s. Now it wasn't a Frankenstein's Monster pastiche like the Hulk who was getting his own series; it was Frankenstein's Monster himself, in *The Monster of Frankenstein*. None other than the Prince of Darkness, Dracula, starred in *Tomb of Dracula*, while a wolf man named Jack Russell appeared in *Werewolf by Night*. Even swamp monsters (*The Man-Thing*), golems (*Strange Tales*), and demon-possessed bikers (*Ghost Rider*) got a chance to shine, while over at DC, ghosts populated World War II battlefields (*Weird War Tales*) and the tales told by the caretakers of various houses and haunts (*Secrets of Haunted House, House of Mystery, House of Secrets*).

But then there were the poor zombies, still battering on the doors and windows, trying to get back into the most visible part of an industry they once dominated. For the grotesque ghouls, there seemed no way to regain a place in the main stage spotlight—or was there?

The zombie subgenre has a long tradition of fearing its own name, with movies and books and games working overtime to come up with new euphemisms like "shamblers," "tanks," and "stenches." *The Walking Dead* has addressed the issue itself, with characters labeling zombies based on their behavior ("walkers," "lurkers," and "roamers"), but decades ago, Marvel Comics pressed this same strategy into service by necessity. The zombies returned to Marvel's paneled pages, but now they were dubbed "zuvembies."

The name wasn't Marvel's creation. The term "zuvembie" had existed as far back as the 1930s, when Conan creator Robert E. Howard introduced female creatures with that name in his story "Pigeons from Hell." Appropriately enough, the label was brought back from beyond the grave to assist the publisher of Conan's comic book exploits, allowing them to sidestep one of the code's remaining restrictions on monster types. This was an odd strategy since the 1971 revision of the code wasn't specific about the name of the creatures at all, but perhaps the fear of renewed code intervention inspired the use of the strange moniker. Marvel's zuvembies rampaged unmolested by censors in titles such as *Strange Tales*, *Brother Voodoo*, and *Marvel Two-in-One*. When the Avengers resurrected a former member, Wonder Man, he too was called a "zuvembie."

There were actual zombies appearing in Marvel titles but only in their line of black-and-white horror magazines that were sheltered from the code, like Gaines' *Mad*, Warren's *Creepy* and *Eerie*, and Skywald's *Psycho*. Marvel's *Tales of the Zombie* starred tortured corpse Simon Garth, resurrected from a one-shot precode appearance in a story by Stan Lee and Bill Everett, "Zombie" (*Menace 5*, July 1953). *Tales of the Zombie* lasted all of ten issues, released between 1973 and 1975.

As with Marvel's magazines, distribution also proved to be the key for DC to circumvent the code for horror titles, though in a much more effective fashion. For much of their history, comics had been sold through newsstands and carried by periodical distribution channels that required books to display the CCA stamp of approval. By the end of the 1970s, even Marvel and DC were selling comics through alternative channels, collectively known as "the direct market," in much the same way the underground publishers had utilized non-traditional distribution to reach their target audience. Comics sold through the direct market were not required to carry the CCA stamp, allowing even the corporate-owned companies to experiment more freely. For DC, this meant a remarkable horror revival under the banner of its Vertigo imprint, with creators such as Neil Gaiman, Alan Moore, and Grant Morrison telling sophisticated and chilling tales in titles such as *Swamp Thing* and *Hellblazer*.

When the CCA code was revised again in 1989, it abandoned specific prohibitions concerning fictional monsters, but by then it hardly mattered. Zombies were appearing in the most mainstream titles in all but name, while the undead had been marauding with impunity in countless alternative, small-press, and independent comics and magazines. The industry had changed so much, thanks to the direct market, that implementation of the code was virtually impossible. The new distribution channels had helped spawn a network of comic book specialty stores that usually welcomed transgressive material, along with a group of independent publishers and creators who were more than ready to take full advantage of the freedom this CCA-less market afforded them.

By the final decades of the twentieth century and the start of the twenty-first, the mavens of morality had for the most part moved on to tackle other all-encompassing threats to the sanctity and sanity of our nation's youth—television, video games, and the internet. Some mainstream critics even acknowledged what others had realized decades ago: comics were capable of great highs and appalling lows like any other medium.

For comics, the road back to the pop culture mainstream started three thousand miles away from the industry's roots in the brownstone and concrete of 1930s New York City. It was a road lined with palm trees and tinsel. Hollywood had always been interested in adapting various colorful comic book heroes to the silver screen, but with the growth of the special effects blockbuster, they turned increasingly toward comics for a wider range of potential projects. Superheroes still accounted for most of the comic-to-movie adaptations, but many other types of stories, from those of teen angst (*Ghost World*) to Academy Award–winning gangster epics (*Road to Perdition*), were translated from print to celluloid (and pixels). With millions of moviegoers validating comic book-related content with their ticket purchases, comics had a renewed reason to stake a claim as an important facet of pop culture.

Through the shift in distribution to the direct market and the proliferation of independent publishers, there were also many more opportunities for comics to push the boundaries beyond the code, even as sales of individual issues dwindled to a fraction of what they were in their heyday. As comics of all kinds circumvented the traditional conduits that led to the code, the CCA was more irrelevant than ever, and only a few companies even bothered to still carry the once-ubiquitous seal on their covers.

Publishers offered everything from edgy reinterpretations of the often staid superhero genre (*The Dark Knight Returns*, *Watchmen*) to deeply personal explorations of history's darkest chapters (*Maus*) to innovative commentaries of sexuality and sociopolitical issues (*Love and Rockets*, *American Flagg!*). And yes, there were intense horror sagas featuring zombies that kept the EC flag flying after Warren's magazines were long gone, including the creator-owned *Deadworld* and Dark Horse's *Zombie World*. Every one of these titles was another chip in the code's already-crumbling wall, and on the other side, the zombies waited for the day when they would take over the mainstream once again.

Into this very different comics industry strode Image Comics, a company composed of former Marvel illustrators eager to make their mark with unique characters and stories that were entirely creator-owned. Launching in 1992 with titles such as *Youngblood* and *Spawn*, Image soon welcomed other creators who brought their own visions to the printed page. In 2003, nearly fifty years after Gaines' fateful testimony, Robert Kirkman pitched a zombie comic book series to Image Comics publisher Jim Valentino. This wasn't to be just a one-shot or a miniseries; his intention was to create the "zombie movie that never ends" in comic book form. It was an ambitious plan to produce a horror comic that would explore all aspects of our current culture through the lens of a postapocalyptic saga filled with ravenous reanimated corpses.

As related in April Snellings' article "My Apocalypse," from the September 2010 issue of *Rue Morgue*, Valentino wasn't so certain the book would work. He was concerned that zombies didn't sell. He was wrong, of course, as zombies were all over pop culture at the time, in movies, short story anthologies, video games, and even comics from publishers such as Dark Horse. But when Kirkman told Valentino his zombie plague was going to be revealed as part of an alien invasion plot, he got the go-ahead to craft the comic of his dreams. A short while later, no one at Image would be mad that Kirkman had lied, much less promised them the plot of *Plan 9 from Outer Space*.

The Walking Dead owes more to zombie movies than it does to other zombie comics. However, there are a few telltale signs of its heritage buried within its mutated DNA, which stretches back to the heady horrors of EC. Every drooling, munching corpse drawn by Tony Moore or Charlie Adlard echoes its cousins crafted by Al Feldstein or Jack Davis decades earlier. The stark cruelty that Kirkman visits upon his ever-changing cast of characters recalls another of Gaines' story requests in that *Writer's Digest* call to action: "we relish the *contes cruels* story." Kirkman's tale employs violence and torture as a means of illuminating aspects of the human condition; in the pages of EC, morality or some deeper theme often played a role in the meting of monstrous justice, but just as often people suffered for the hell of it, for the visceral thrill. Such is progress in the realm of horror comics.

In the aftermath of *The Walking Dead*'s success, Kirkman helped to bring zombies—not zuvembies—to the Marvel Universe en masse in one of the most popular comic miniseries of the last twenty years. Following their introduction by Mark Millar in the pages of *Ultimate Fantastic Four*, the Kirkman-scripted *Marvel Zombies* miniseries inspired several sequels, and DC followed with its own take on super-zombies via its *Blackest Night* crossover series. While Marvel's undead were the result of a viral infection, DC's walking corpses were reanimated by death-powered Black Lantern rings. In 2011, IDW Publishing offered a crossover saga called *Infestation*, pitting zombies against the licensed worlds of *Transformers*, *G.I. Joe*, *Ghostbusters*, and *Star Trek*. In the new landscape of comic book publishing, zombies have never been more widespread or unstoppable.

In January 2011, fifty-seven years after the Comic Book Code was first implemented, Archie Comics became the last of the major American comic book publishers to drop the code and its almost nonexistent aura of approval. The company that had helped establish the code was now the publisher to drive the final nail in its coffin. At the same time, zombies have reached an unprecedented level of mainstream popularity. As the Comic Book Code itself is laid to rest with little fanfare, the creatures that the code tried to bury forever have emerged from their crypts and clawed their way to the top of the comic book pantheon. This time they aren't vilified for corrupting our sensitive minds but celebrated for their contribution to a deeper understanding of our culture.

As for horror comics specifically, titles such as *The Walking Dead* and its many creepy cohorts demonstrate the ability of even the most abhorred genres of the past to serve a vital purpose and throw an allegorical spotlight on humankind. This plague is sure to spread. With luck, the walking dead will march on, seducing the innocent with their unique and potent blend of horror and cogent social commentary.

ARNOLD T. BLUMBERG is an author, book designer, and educator. He has written numerous books and articles on genre entertainment and pop culture history. He co-authored *Zombiemania: 80 Movies to Die For*, contributed to the *Doctor Who: Short Trips* series, and writes for IGN.com and AssignmentX.com. He teaches a course on zombies in popular media at the University of Baltimore that garnered worldwide press coverage, as well as courses on comic book and time travel literature at the University of Maryland. He sometimes checks to see how fast he can unlock his door in case of a sudden zombie apocalypse. Online at atbpublishing.com.

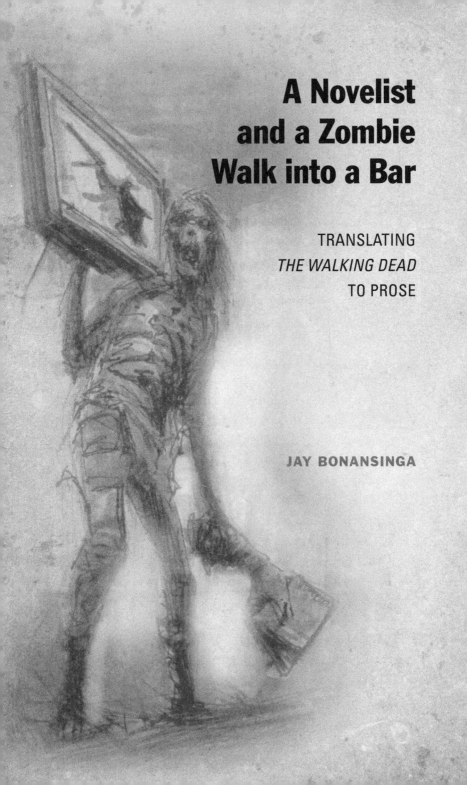

A Novelist
and a Zombie
Walk into a Bar

TRANSLATING
THE WALKING DEAD
TO PROSE

JAY BONANSINGA

A dear friend, who also happens to be a Hollywood talent manager, rings me up one day last summer and babbles into the phone: "Some people I know are shopping for a novelist to help write a book based on a comic that's being developed into a TV series. You with me so far?"

I mumble something like, "Um . . . I think so."

"Anyway," he goes on, "you would be working with the guy who created the comic, who is somewhat of a big shot, and you know, this deal could very possibly open many doors across the southern region of California. And when I heard they were looking for some author with horror chops who can play nice with others and has a really sick, disgusting imagination and is somewhat morally challenged . . . I naturally thought of you."

"Uh huh," I say. "And may I be so impertinent as to ask the name of the comic?"

"Ever hear of *The Walking Dead?*"

"The Norman Mailer book?"

"That's *The Naked and the Dead* . . . and I said comic."

"There aren't any naked people in this?"

"Are you on something right now?"

"I'm kidding." I take a deep breath. "Of course I've heard of *The Walking Dead* . . . cripes! Who do you think I am, your dad? It won the Eisner Award and it's like a marathon of great, lost Romero movies all strung together . . . but better . . . it's like the picture George Romero would make in heaven on acid with God as his cinematographer."

After a long, exasperated pause, my buddy says, "Shall I take that as a *Yes, you're interested?*"

Robert Kirkman's epic survival saga *The Walking Dead* lives in its own graphic stratosphere—a rarefied yet austere visual canvas that screams out for translation into other media. Among the iconic roster of superstars who have rushed in to decode Kirkman's muscular visual universe are Hollywood luminaries Frank Darabont and Gale Anne Hurd, whose basic-cable phenomenon of the same name pulls off a major coup: it captures the human drama beneath all the rotting flesh and ultimately channels the power of Kirkman's two-dimensional frames into the bland, parochial world of the small screen.

Producers of the mega-smash AMC TV series have made two important discoveries: 1) the spiritual center of the comic series—a human story playing out amid all the gore—translates well to the intimate confines of television; and 2) the ingenious way Kirkman builds big cliffhanger moments into splash pages that end each issue works like gangbusters on the tube. After a fleeting first season of only six episodes—an introduction to the Kirkman universe so ephemeral it almost seems like a freak accident—viewers were hungrier than reanimated corpses for more red meat.

Now we come to the second re-imagining of *The Walking Dead*, a trilogy of all-original novels based on Kirkman's mythos, which take readers deeper into the narrative waters and all the rich tributaries branching out of the central story. Commissioned to coincide with the highly anticipated second season of the AMC series—premiering on Halloween 2011—the books are the latest milestone in the media crossover sensation.

In some ways I feel as though I was born to collaborate with Mr. Kirkman. A film school brat, I was weaned on EC comics—*Vault of Horror, Tales from the Crypt*, et al.—and after graduating, I spent years writing short horror stories for magazines such as *Grue, Cemetery Dance*, and *Weird Tales*.

After publishing my first novel, *The Black Mariah*, in 1994, I had the absolute sublime pleasure of working with George Romero on the film adaptation of said book. I will never forget landing at the Fort Myers airport for a story meeting at George's house in Florida and seeing this big, burly grizzly bear of a man loping toward me with a huge smile. "Let me carry that," he said, eyeing my suitcase. I was aghast and euphoric in equal parts. The thought of my childhood hero schlepping my luggage was my first lesson in a strange dichotomy: those who create the darkest, nastiest, harshest fictions are in true life the biggest pussycats.

Robert Kirkman is no exception. After working with him on the first installment in this triptych, I am stunned by how gracious, humble, and down-to-earth the man is. But the more I think about it, the more I conclude that this kind of unexpected sweetness—as is the case with George Romero—is Kirkman's secret weapon.

This decency and plainspoken nature is actually what has enabled Robert Kirkman to reinvent an entire genre in comic book form.

After encountering the *Walking Dead* comics, no reader will ever be able to watch a zombie film, or read a zombie story, or just generally think of zombies in quite the same way. Without spoiling the main narrative for anyone living under the proverbial rock, suffice it to say that the comic paints a familiar picture with unfamiliar colors and tones. In the early issues, a small ragtag band of everypeople find themselves struggling to survive an inexplicable plague of cannibalistic, reanimated corpses. But the thing that instantly sinks a hook into readers—and is probably responsible for turning the comic into a milestone of the genre—is an unexpected humanity.

The characters of *The Walking Dead* are not mere characters; they are people. They are terrified, and they are morally sickened, and they long for deliverance, and they love their children, and they will do anything to protect their families. In other words, unlike the marionettes of most zombie books and movies, these people act like . . . well . . . *real people.*

"So . . . you got a name?" the lonely main character, Rick Grimes, whimsically asked a horse on which he rode through a desolate landscape in an early issue. The former police officer had just awakened from a coma after being shot in the line of duty, and now he was frantically searching the apocalyptic byways for his family. "I held her hand the *whole* time," Grimes later recounted for the uncomprehending animal, describing his wife's labor and the subsequent birth of his son. "There were some complications . . . and she had to get a *cesarean*. I was really worried . . ." Grimes eventually chokes on the words and can't go on . . . but in a way he discovers right then why he *must* go on . . . and why we the readers must turn the page!

This is the keystone of *The Walking Dead*'s power: an unexpected tenderness in the characters. Because of this, the stakes of this story are raised incrementally with each page. You care a little bit more. You empathize. And, perhaps most importantly, you realize that this empathy is what makes the next eruption of trademark zombie-splatter all the more horrific.

Kirkman and his team of artists keep the visual strategy of the comic simple and linear. The style brings to mind the kitchen-sink realism of Bernie Wrightson of *Swamp Thing* and Warren horror comics fame. Both literary and filmic devices are put to good use. As is silence: characters brood and ruminate word-lessly in many of the panels, often captioned by a simple and inscrutable ellipsis. At other points, the comic's mise-en-scène of epic filmmaking conjures memories of Sergio Leone and David Lean. Intimate close-ups widen out to panoramic landscapes of vast prison yards and urban outskirts. Huge empty skies are stitched with Hitchcockian crows.

The Walking Dead begs comparison to both EC horror and end-of-the-world epics such as *Earth Abides*, *The Stand*, and *I Am Legend*, but, more than anything else, it is the character-driven pathos that truly elevates the series into transcendent territory. It is also the thing that fuels the adaptation Robert and I tackled in the early months of 2011.

I wish I could say we labored with Sisyphean effort to translate the panel-bound world of the *Walking Dead* comic into the ethereal, cerebral, non-linear world of prose. I wish I could say we ingeniously contorted the visual details of the comic book into exotic allegories and literary equivalents. But the truth is, the mythos of *The Walking Dead* made the leap to fiction with the ease of a bullet passing through the rotten gray matter of an animated corpse. Maybe this was due to the relentless forward motion of Kirkman's narrative. Perhaps it was because of the meticulous simplicity of the plot—every twist, every turn, every shift in point of view, every "money shot" completely, utterly motivated.

Technically a comic book's closest cousin is the feature film. In a movie, a story is told with pictures and dialogue. Things happen, and people react to those things ... and everything occurs in the here and now, with minimal, if any, use of devices such as flashback (a staple of prose). Of course, there are movies that employ voice-over narration—think of Philip Marlowe recalling how dark and stormy the night was when that crazy dame walked through his door—but, again, such devices are actually quite rare. Even in the case of movies with a narrator, the main body of the story unfolds in the present tense.

Such is also the case with the comic book medium. Granted, there are occasional thought bubbles, as well as boxes and side-bars containing Godlike, omniscient narration, but for the most part, comics—especially modern comics—*show* rather than *tell*. Instead of revealing a character's thoughts (or providing clunky, whimsical narration in the style of the Crypt-Keeper), the modern comic shows you *internal* life through *external* action. *The Walking Dead* abides by this axiom with almost religious fervor. Nobody pauses to think . . . they just *do*. They love, they hate, they struggle, they dream, they plot, they screw up, they live, they die, they kick zombie ass, they get devoured . . . all of it in real time.

Here's the kicker: Despite the inherent differences between comics and prose, Kirkman and I found the act of rendering *The Walking Dead* into a novel fascinatingly expedient. The way the visual flow of the comic is organized cries out for analogous organization in a book. The cliffhanger splash pages suggest twist endings to chapters. The density of panoramic landscapes leads to cinematic scene-setting. The gruesome detail of cadaverous faces and all the vivid carnage demands visceral description. And Kirkman's lean, straightforward way with dialogue looks and sounds terrific on the printed page—a mixture of Cormac McCarthy and Martin Scorsese.

Conventional wisdom says that novels—unlike movies, television, comics, or theater—are internal. You get *inside* the thoughts and motives of the characters. In novels you are free to present your story in non-linear fashion, jumping back and forth in time and point of view. Novels are digital rather than analog. They are everywhere all at once. They are impressionistic rather than structural. To put it another way, a novel is *inside-out* instead of *outside-in*. You tell your story from *inside* the characters, and the power comes from an accumulation of detail.

Even the action-oriented adventure books of yesteryear— beginning with the turn-of-the-century penny dreadfuls and continuing through the pulps of the 1950s—told their stories through the steely nervous systems of their lantern-jawed heroes. Granted, the internal stream-of-consciousness of a Doc Savage or a Conan the Barbarian were not exactly grist for Freudian analysis. But the form itself necessitated that the reader feel the sting of a poison-tipped spear from *inside* the synapses of the hero.

On a deeper level, the novel can also be about something else altogether. In this chaotic age of the internet, gaming, and social networking, the novel—more than ever—is the most interactive of all media. It is about getting inside the thoughts and motives of the *reader*. Subtly, insidiously, sensually, sneakily, the novel is all about touching off the flames of the imagination.

As William Burroughs said, "Language is a virus from outer space." And what a good novel does is infect the *inner* space of a reader with images, sounds, smells, tastes, and textures.

Happily, the universe of *The Walking Dead* is not only born out of a very direct, linear approach to narrative, but is also evocative of myriad sights, sounds, smells, tastes, and textures— most of which are latent, hiding within the panels, alluded to in the dialogue, suggested by the narrative.

The fictional version teases these sensory details into the foreground. A reader is spared nothing. The senses are assaulted by the side effects of the plague. Explanations are eschewed in favor of a constant triangulation of sensory input. A floor is sticky

with gore, giving off an oily black aroma as the characters investigate a deserted room buzzing with the vibrations of bluebottle
flies and the echo of something moaning in the basement.

This profusion of sensory detail ultimately dictated the sty-
listic approach that Kirkman and I adopted for the novels.

Not only do the *Walking Dead* novels move with the inertia
of a fever dream—all told in the present tense, jumping from
one point of view to another with the quick-cut velocity of a
movie montage—but the sensory details suggested in the panels
of the comic are amplified, intensified, enriched. Like particles
charged with radioactive half-lives, the flies on a corpse lead to
internal trauma among eyewitnesses, which leads to madness,
which leads to the slaughter of more corpses and the geometric
population growth of flies. The world now has flies on it, the
core of civilization rotting from the inside, personified by the
internal atrophy of the characters. And always at the center
of the action is the single most important symbol, the engine
powering the conflict from the inside as well as the outside,
the moldering, festering raison d'être around which everything
revolves, the key to the whole damn thing . . .

The zombie.

As a novelist, I cut my teeth during the horror boom of the
1980s—that heady time when anything with a lurid foil cover
and the words "evil" or "phantom" in the title ruled the bestseller
list with the consistency of death and taxes. I learned to write
by gobbling up Stephen King, Peter Straub, Clive Barker, Joe
Lansdale, David Schow, and Skipp & Spector. And I started
getting published at the cusp of the splatter-punk bubble, when
guys like Edward Lee and Rex Miller were pushing the envelope
of anatomically incorrect gore. But I think the greatest influences

on my writing were the archetypes of supernatural horror: ghosts, vampires, werewolves, demons, and manmade monsters of all makes and models.

Popularized first in the classic Universal Studios films of the 1930s and 1940s, these mythological beings have been cash cows for nearly a century. But historically, their origins go back all the way to the nineteenth century, springing from the quill pens and genteel sensibilities of Mary Shelley and Bram Stoker.

On the page, the archetypes have aged well because they have deeper meanings than mere bogeymen. The vampire—a potent symbol of repressed human sexuality—finds new and romantic iterations in teenybopper romances such as *Twilight*. The devil and his minions—those pesky personifications of our baser instincts—are alive and well in works such as William Peter Blatty's *The Exorcist*. Ghosts—our stubborn, guilty past consuming the present—continue to haunt literature, both highbrow and low. But what about the lowly, hapless zombie? How does this archetype fit in? What does a zombie represent culturally? Why hasn't it enjoyed more days in the literary sun? One is hard pressed to name a zombie classic in book form. Stephen King's *Cell*? Max Brooks' *World War Z*? These are fine books, but I'm not sure we have yet seen a literary zombie masterpiece . . . and the reason may be as simple as the problem of comparing oranges to rotten apples.

The zombie is the coin of the *visual* realm—a conceit of movies and comic books. By design, the archetype has no "there" there—zombies are eating machines, dead inside and out, with no purpose other than devouring the living and multiplying. Even their appearance has a sort of uniform, machine-stamped quality—albeit a gruesome one—that brings to mind the way death makes us all the same. Namely . . . gross and inert.

Keep in mind that I'm not referring here to the gothic voodoo wraith as depicted in subtle cinema such as Val Lewton's *I Walked with a Zombie*. I'm talking about George Romero's lurid concoction first unleashed on the war-weary, turbulent, paranoid society of the late 1960s. The rainbow coalition of shambling, slow-moving, cannibal roamers in *Night of the Living Dead* resonated deeply in the American imagination over the next four decades . . . and they resonated for a reason.

Romero's zombies represent the wolves at our doors. They represent your mortgage, your car payments, your pending divorce, the suspicious lump under your skin—the things that just keep coming at you and will not stop until you are toast. Xenophobia, the collapse of society, your toilet backing up—these are the dream symbols personified by the undead.

Robert Kirkman knows this well. In his comics he constructs a human underground fighting to retain its humanity in the face of the wolf pack—and the moldering beasts just keep on coming and coming, as inexhaustible as cancer cells. The depiction of the zombies in *The Walking Dead* are lavish, Grand Guignol works of art. The sunken faces are lovingly rendered, the hollow cheeks and blank eyes carefully delineated to distinguish one monster from another. It's like a nightmarish catalogue of exotic fighting fish.

And this is the key to our translation.

Until Robert Kirkman decides to include scratch-and-sniff panels on his comics, the non-visual senses will be the stars of their prose counterpart. Through meticulously calibrated description, we layer the smells and sounds and textures. This is how we translate something that is purely visual, by writing it in "odorama"—getting inside the senses of the readers. In other words, in the purely visual world of the comic, we must *see* Rick Grimes reacting to an odor—"Phew!"—in order for us to smell that odor. In the novels, we go straight for the nose.

Have you ever wondered what a warehouse filled with hundreds of upright cadavers would really smell like? Or have you thought about what a chorus of thousands of zombies all moaning at the same time would sound like? Maybe you've ruminated about what the exact texture of brain matter is like after getting sprayed across the inside of a windshield.

Doesn't everybody wonder about these things?

The best part of this sensory feast, however, is for those who hunger to go deeper into *The Walking Dead* backstories. The trilogy—the first installment of which is available from St. Martin's Press—is no mere tie-in. These are not standard novelizations that follow a screenplay or comic note for note. *Our* books—courtesy of the endless well of Kirkman's fecund imagination—explore the origins of mysterious characters and the tantalizing secrets and relationships only alluded to or fleetingly glimpsed in the comics.

As a novelist, I could not ask for a more exciting thrill ride.

Six months after that original call from my Hollywood friend in which he floated the idea of going on this amazing journey with Robert Kirkman, my pal calls me back. "Hey, Boopie," he says. "How's the zombie business?"

"We're killing 'em in Poughkeepsie," I tell him.

"What stage are you at?"

"I'm close to writing 'The End,'" I say. "Right now I'm in a warehouse full of dead people."

"What's it smell like in there?" he asks.

"You don't want to know."

"C'mon, I can take it."

"Okay. It smells like a combination of human feces and bacon cooked in pus."

After a long pause—during which I can hear a faint gagging

noise—he says, "God, I hate you . . . I have a lunch meeting today at Greenblatt's Deli, and had planned on the chicken liver."

"You asked."

"I'll have that smell in my schnoz for weeks."

He cannot see me smiling. "That's the idea, my friend . . . that's the idea."

JAY BONANSINGA is a national bestselling author, screenwriter, and filmmaker, whose directorial debut, *Stash*, premiered in 2010. His 2005 novel, *Frozen*, is in development as a major motion picture, and his latest book, *Perfect Victim*, is an alternate title for Book-of-the-Month Club. He has worked with George Romero and has won major film festival awards, including a Gold Remi at the Houston International WorldFest and a "Best Comedy Feature" at the Iowa City Landlocked Film Festival. Jay's 2004 nonfiction debut, *The Sinking of the Eastland*, won the Certificate of Merit from the Illinois State Historical Society, and his forthcoming nonfiction Civil War thriller, *Pinkerton's War*, is due out from Lyons Press in late 2011. Online at jaybonansinga.com.

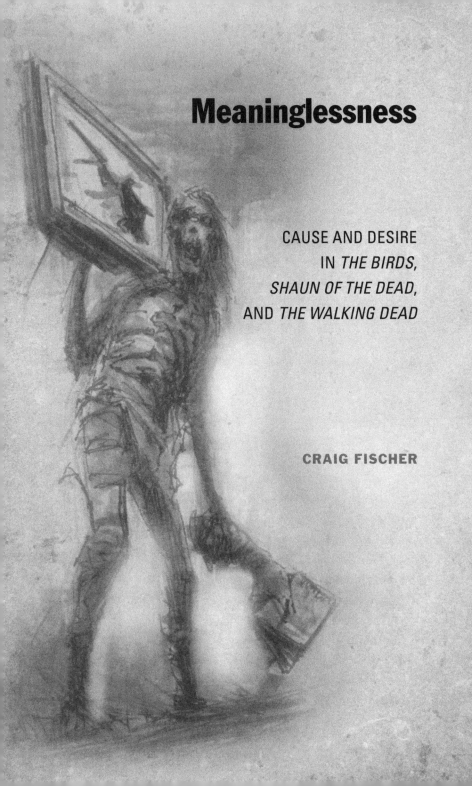

Meaninglessness

CAUSE AND DESIRE
IN *THE BIRDS*,
SHAUN OF THE DEAD,
AND *THE WALKING DEAD*

CRAIG FISCHER

n both its comic book and television incarnations, *The Walking Dead* asks a fundamental narrative question: Why do the dead come back to life? This is a question posed by other entries in the zombie subgenre too, most notably George Romero's series of six zombie films (from 1968's *Night of the Living Dead* to 2009's *Survival of the Dead*), none of which offer an explanation for the epidemic beyond the pseudo-biblical "when there is no more room in Hell, the dead will walk the earth" dialogue from *Dawn of the Dead* (1978). Some individual zombie movies, however, hint at deeper psychological causes behind the zombie apocalypse; some give us a protagonist whose unconscious desires are so ferocious that they bring back the dead and reshape the world.

To explore this desire-driven category of the subgenre, I begin with a long look at Alfred Hitchcock's *The Birds* (1963)—not explicitly a zombie film, of course, but a profound influence on George Romero and later chroniclers of zombie catastrophes. Next, I discuss Edgar Wright's *Shaun of the Dead* (2004) as a contemporary example of a zombie movie in which unconscious desires drive the carnage and the plot. Then I turn to the subjects of this anthology—Robert Kirkman, Tony Moore, and Charlie Adlard's *The Walking Dead* comic book and Frank Darabont's TV adaptation of *The Walking Dead*—and argue that both versions are a *critique* of the desire-driven zombie film. *The Birds* and *Shaun* posit reasons, however metaphorical and uncanny, for their apocalypses; *The Walking Dead*, however, presents a world stripped of higher meaning and existential purpose, where characters desperately try, and fail, to find causal connections among themselves, their expressed and repressed desires, and the zombie whirlwind.

For me, *The Birds* is a proto-zombie film, a movie that establishes many of the conventions for both Romero's *Dead* series and *The Walking Dead*. The attacking birds serve the same function in Hitchcock's film as zombies do in *Night of the Living Dead*: both birds and zombies become inscrutable marauders, creatures that deviate from behavior we take for granted in order to assault and feast on living humans. After all, birds are supposed to be docile, and dead people are supposed to remain, well, dead.

Another trait shared by *The Birds* and the subsequent zombie subgenre is an emphasis on architecture. As Hitchcock's birds show their capacity for savagery, the characters become obsessed with shelter, constantly evaluating the safest places to be during a bird attack. A young girl is in danger because her school has long, tall windows, and the central protagonist, Melanie Daniels, flees into a phone booth to protect herself—and unwittingly finds herself "caged," like the lovebirds she buys at the beginning of the film. This architectural focus crops up in later zombie films, and sometimes even specific images are repeated: the shots from *The Birds* of Mitch Brenner nailing planks across the front door of his family home become the scenes of barricaded doors—with undead hands and arms crashing through—in *Night of the Living Dead*, which in turn become Morgan's locked and nailed-shut front door in the first episode of the *Walking Dead* TV show.

Given that architecture and shelter are essential to survival in these catastrophe-tossed worlds, it's not surprising that many zombie films give us high-angle, maplike establishing shots that reveal zones of danger and safety. Perhaps the most famous shot in *The Birds* occurs after the gas station in Bodega Bay explodes and Hitchcock cuts to an extreme high-angle aerial view of the town, the gas fire slashing across its main road like a wound. (Gradually, birds fly into the shot and then descend to strike.) *Night of the Living Dead* likewise includes a gas explosion and shots from a helicopter near the end of the film, as the redneck vigilantes scour the countryside, looking for zombies to kill. In *Dawn of the Dead*, Romero offers more aerial views, most notably of the mall that provides *Dawn*'s helicopter-hijacking characters with semipermanent sanctuary. Borrowing from *Dawn*, issue twelve of the *Walking Dead* comic concludes with a double-page long shot of West Central Prison, as Rick and his group gaze down at the facility from a hillside and Rick tells everyone, "Look at all the land *inside* the fence . . . safe, secure. We could make a *life* here." And so they do, until issue forty-eight and the Governor's onslaught. The high-angle shot in *The Birds* shows the extent of the threat, while the prison vista in *The Walking Dead* offers a possible safe haven, but both emphasize how important knowledge of your environment is when the natural order goes murderously awry.

But careful readers will already object: *The Birds* isn't the only nature-gone-mad film concerned with claustrophobic shelter and establishing shots. What about a movie like, say, Ray Kellogg's Z-grade *The Killer Shrews* (1959), in which mutated giant shrews attack humans hiding in a shack? (These humans escape by welding together a portable shelter made of metal barrels and walking in these barrels down to a pier, where they then flee by boat.) The difference is in *The Birds*' parallel plot, the love triangle between Melanie Daniels, Mitch Brenner, and Mitch's mother, Lydia Brenner. *The Birds* is named after the avian attacks on Bodega Bay, a small California beach town, but the center of our attention is Melanie Daniels, a beautiful socialite who meets lawyer Mitch Brenner in a San Francisco pet shop. After a flirty skirmish with Mitch, Melanie impulsively researches Mitch's background, buys a pair of lovebirds as a present for him, and drives to Bodega Bay, Mitch's hometown, to drop the birds off. After Melanie pilots a boat to the Brenner homestead—during which she is dive-bombed by a single bird—Mitch invites Melanie home for dinner. The situation in the Brenner household is tense; Mitch lives with his adolescent sister, Cathy, and widowed mother, and it soon becomes clear that Lydia is unnaturally dependent on Mitch and resents Melanie's potential to lure Mitch away from home. Against Lydia's preference, Melanie spends the night in Bodega Bay (with Annie, one of Mitch's ex-girlfriends) and is attending a birthday party for Cathy when the bird blitzkrieg begins in earnest.

Are the bird attacks and the Melanie-Mitch plotline somehow connected? Some believe that the savagery of the birds is a palpable manifestation of Lydia's anger over Melanie's presence in Bodega Bay. In a 1963 interview with Peter Bogdanovich, Hitchcock himself bluntly admitted that Lydia "has been substituting her son for her husband," a fact reinforced by the film's bizarre casting—Jessica Tandy (Lydia) looks like a slightly older version of Tippi Hedren (Melanie) and seems too young to play Rod Taylor's (Mitch's) mother. (There's a similar mother-son disconnect in Hitchcock's *North by Northwest* [1959], in which Jessie Royce Landis, age sixty-three, plays the mother of fifty-five-year-old Cary Grant, and troubled, sexualized mother-son issues are, of course, at the heart of *Psycho* [1960].) Slavoj Žižek, an important psychoanalytic critic of Hitchcock, argues that the birds are a living metaphor for the unspoken yet barely sublimated Oedipal desire between Lydia and Mitch. In the hilarious documentary *The Pervert's Guide to Cinema* (2006), Žižek digitally inserts himself into various movies—including

The Matrix (1999) and *Mulholland Drive* (2001)—to explicate his Freudian-Lacanian theories about cinema as a medium. As he invades the world of *The Birds*, taking Melanie's place on the one-person motorboat headed to the Brenner home, Žižek defines the Melanie-Mitch-Lydia situation as "the standard Oedipal imbroglio of incestuous tension between the mother and son, with the son split between his possessive mother and the intrusive girl." He then poses the "stupid, obvious" question about the movie: "Why do the birds attack?" His answer includes some jargon-laden speculations about threats to the "Symbolic order," but for our purposes, the reasons boil down to this: "The violent attacks of the birds are obviously explosive outbursts of maternal superego—of the maternal figure trying to prevent a sexual relationship. So the birds are raw, incestuous energy." Specifically, they are a manifestation of Lydia's raw, incestuous energy, a metaphor powerful enough to alter the story world that the characters inhabit.

Žižek's interpretation veers close to Stephen King territory: in such books (and movies) as *Carrie* and *The Dead Zone*, King creates lead characters with supernatural abilities and then drops them in difficult circumstances (what could be more hellish than high school and American politics?) that test both their new powers and their fragile mental states. The difference is that Carrie White and Johnny Smith are explicitly identified as "gifted," while Lydia Brenner's summoning of the birds is implied—and, in my opinion, all the more unsettling for viewers because this cause remains unexplained and oblique. Because of the Hollywood Production Code, which was waning quickly but still able to exert regulation on Hollywood mainstream films of the early 1960s, Lydia's "raw, incestuous energy" went unspoken and remained repressed, a sea of waves rolling beneath the surface of *The Birds*' narrative.

A more recent film, this one explicitly in the zombie subgenre, uses an apocalypse to resolve tensions among a woman, a man, and the man's mother. *Shaun of the Dead* begins as dysfunctional couple Shaun and Liz sit in the Winchester Pub, wasting away. The first shot is a close-up on Shaun, drinking and smoking, as the bartender calls, "Last orders, please." Very soon after, Liz delivers her last orders to Shaun, begging his help in reigniting their relationship:

> Shaun, what I'm trying to say is—I need more. Rather than spending every night in the Winchester, I wanna get out there and do more interesting stuff. I wanna live a little, and I want you to want to do it too. Ooh, listen to me—I'm beginning to sound like your mum. Not that I know what she sounds like . . .

What follows is a whirl of Oedipal confusion, as it becomes clear that Shaun has lived in a state of unresolved adolescence: he has avoided introducing Liz, his girlfriend of more than three years, to his mother, and he doesn't get along with his stepfather. After Shaun bungles a restaurant reservation, Liz declares that she has to "do something," or else "I'm gonna end up in that pub every night for the rest of my life." Cut to another close-up of Shaun as Liz breaks up with him and kicks him out of her apartment building; the breakup is ostensibly her "something," but the ominous thunder on the soundtrack also heralds the imminent zombie apocalypse, a catastrophe that remakes Shaun into an action hero while simultaneously resolving his Oedipal issues. Shaun has heart-to-heart conversations with both his mother and his stepfather before they die, and his undead flatmate, Ed, is even exiled to the shed by the end of the movie, displaced as Liz's primary rival for Shaun's attention. Like Lydia, Liz gets what she wants.

The tone of Kirkman, Moore, and Adlard's comic is worlds away from the gore slapstick of *Shaun of the Dead*, but another important difference is that *The Walking Dead* explores permutations of desire other than the Oedipal triangles of *The Birds* and *Shaun*. Besides the many heterosexual relationships throughout the series, there is the non-incestuous love triangle among Michonne, Tyreese, and Carol, which begins as soon as Michonne enters the comic, in issue nineteen, and Carol's later offer of an open marriage three-way with Rick and Lori in issue twenty-seven. Also present is a focus on expressed and repressed male, rather than female, desire. Scenes and plotlines throughout the series present male characters trying—and failing—to link their own passions to the undead apocalypse and thus tap into the power that Lydia and Liz unconsciously channel in *The Birds* and *Shaun*. In issue thirteen, for instance, Rick and his band of survivors arrive at West Central Prison, where they encounter several convicts holed up in the cells, including Andrew, a smack user who believes that the zombie plague was God's way of curing his addiction. In a long vertical panel at the bottom of a page, Andrew says:

> So I turned to *God*—if you can believe it. I asked him—*begged him*—to please, help get me off that smack. I wanted to go clean, once and for all . . . I knew I wouldn't be able to do it without *his* help. So I *asked* him—and the *next day* the news reports started. *Now* look at me. I'm completely clean. I couldn't—I couldn't get my hands on anything if I *tried*.

The two panels at the top of the next page are identical close-ups on Rick and his wife, Lori. There are no words in the first panel, and in the second, Rick speaks, quickly changing the topic: "*Okay*. So—uh, how did you guys end up *stuck* in here?"

The effect is that of a double-take; Rick and Lori are incredulous that this junkie thinks that he has brought about the end of the world, and so are we. Kirkman's zombie apocalypse—unlike those of *The Birds* and *Shaun*—is arbitrary, despite Andrew's attempt to invest it with personal meaning.

Future events validate their skepticism. Unlike Lydia and Liz, who unwittingly unleash catastrophes and emotionally profit because of them, Andrew is an early victim of the new zombie order. Andrew and alpha prisoner Dexter had a sexual relationship while in prison, and as tensions escalate between Rick's group and the prisoners, Andrew remains loyal to Dexter, smuggling guns out of the guard center to arm his fellow prisoners. After Rick shoots Dexter during the confusion of a zombie attack, however, Andrew flees from the prison and out of the series.

According to the *Walking Dead* wiki, Kirkman says that "Andrew died somewhere along the way" after leaving the prison, his fate indicated not in the comic itself but in the fact that the CS Moore Studio created a "torso statuette" of Andrew as a zombie for the 2008 Emerald City Comicon. This is a minor example of how *The Walking Dead* partakes in what Henry Jenkins calls "convergence culture": the marketing of a single narrative across multiple media platforms, with important information given in such "fringe" media as statuettes and video games and not repeated in affiliated films and text. In other words, Andrew dies "offstage," after staking the self-important claim that it's his prayer for sobriety that causes the zombie plague. Andrew is inconsequential; Rick and Lori mock his ideas, and he never becomes a significant, potent presence in *The Walking Dead*, as Lydia and Liz are in their stories. In Robert Kirkman's zombie world, Andrew's beliefs in prayer and agency are delusions.

The other character who purports to know the secret of the zombie apocalypse is Eugene Porter, a scientist introduced in issue fifty-three. Porter says he knows "*exactly* what caused this mess" and hints that the zombie plague is a result of the United States government "weaponizing" the human genome and "developing diseases that would only affect people of a certain . . . regional background." Porter also claims that Washington has the "infra-structure" to cure the zombie disease and restore normalcy, and for a time Rick's group and other survivors troop toward Washington. In issue sixty-seven, however, Porter is exposed as an obscure high school science teacher, spreading lies to make himself indispensable to post-zombie survivalist groups. Once again, knowledge about the origin of the zombie apocalypse is shown to be the fantasy of a weak male character.

A stronger male figure whose desires are at the core of the *Walking Dead* story is Shane Walsh, Rick's partner in the police department. Shane has adored Lori for a long time, despite her marriage to Rick. Rick is shot in a gun battle, falls into a coma, and is hospitalized; then the zombie plague breaks out, and Shane travels to Atlanta with Rick's wife and son, Carl. A flashback in issue seven shows Shane and Lori's single night of intimacy, with Shane whispering, "Oh, Lori . . . I've wanted this for so long." Shane's long-deferred desire for Lori might be the unconscious cause of the catastrophe, the male sex drive dis-placed into the wholesale *Thanatos* of zombie cannibalism.

The Walking Dead, however, treats Shane as a weak char-acter, as opposed to the central women in *The Birds* and *Shaun*. In *The Birds*, Lydia is triumphant. Melanie is driven to catatonia by the attacks, and the film ends with Lydia helping Melanie into a getaway car, stroking her hair and treating her like a daughter, a move that strips Melanie, at least temporarily, of her status as a sexual rival and potential mate for Mitch. Liz in *Shaun* also gets her way: Shaun proves his ability to transcend slacker lethargy, the zombie threat is normalized (note the satirical clips of zombies on game and talk shows at the end of the film), and Shaun and Liz settle into a comfortable domesticity. In *The Walking Dead*, however, Shane's emotions lead to his death. From the moment Rick reunites with Lori and Carl, Shane simmers with resentment, until he erupts at the conclusion to issue six, muttering, "She would have come around eventually," and raising his rifle to shoot Rick. Carl saves his father by shooting Shane in the neck, and Shane dies. The zombie outbreak ultimately does *not* give Shane possession of Lori.

Although Shane is dead, his influence continues to permeate the series. In issue fifteen, Rick processes his ambivalent feelings about Shane by digging up Shane's now-reanimated corpse, calling him a "good man," blasting a bullet through zombie Shane's head, and exiting the scene with the line "I ain't gonna bury you *again*, you son of a *bitch*." Rick and Lori also cope with the fact that the one-night tryst between Lori and Shane made Lori pregnant. In issue thirty-eight, the couple refuses to discuss the baby's paternity. "I finally understand," Rick says. "I just don't need to hear you *say* it. I can't hear you say it." Shane exerts more power dead than alive: for Lori and Rick, Shane's death represents the painful but practical realization that human passions can be more extreme, and human betrayal can be deadly, in the new zombie order. It's a trauma that remains primary in Rick's consciousness, until a more traumatic event supersedes it—the murder of Lori and her newly born child, Judith, during the Governor's assault on West Central Prison.

The first season of the *Walking Dead* TV show tacks in a different direction. The *Walking Dead* fans came to the show with certain expectations—primarily, that Shane would be shot sometime during the first six episodes, just as he was in issue six of the comic. But instead Shane survives, and the show enters its second season with the Rick-Lori-Shane triangle intact. ("Wildfire," the fifth episode of the *Walking Dead*'s first season, flirts with a version of the comic book scene. We see Shane secretly aim his rifle at Rick during a quiet moment in the woods but then decide not to shoot.) This variation is designed to keep both casual viewers and previous *Walking Dead* fans involved in the show. Those audience members familiar only with the TV show won't notice or care about the differences between the comics and the show, and undoubtedly the *Walking Dead* producer Frank Darabont hopes that keeping Shane alive will add soap-opera juice to the second season. In the same dramatic spirit, Darabont foregrounds the issue of Lori's pregnancy (and the identity of the father) sooner than in the comics—assuming that in the sixth episode the secret that Centers for Disease Control scientist Edwin Jenner whispers in Rick's ear is about the result of Lori's blood test.

By keeping Shane in the narrative, Darabont alters the *Walking Dead* franchise in some fascinating ways. For fans, the differences between the *Walking Dead* comics and show are very much in line with those of other franchises and reboots. In a world of multiple Batmans—including different comic books for kids and older fans, the live-action films of the eighties and nineties, the more contemporary Christopher Nolan movies, TV shows such as the Adam West camp-fest, and animated cartoons such as *The Brave and the Bold*—fans will find it easy to keep the comics and TV versions of *The Walking Dead* separate and will have fun debating the differences on *Walking Dead* message boards and fan sites. I too prefer a TV series of unexpected deviations from Kirkman's narrative over a predictable treatment of the source material.

More importantly, Darabont opens up the possibility that the plague is, in fact, caused by Shane's illicit love for Lori. In episode six, we see a flashback in which Shane behaves heroically: he visits Rick in the hospital and is unable to disconnect the comatose Rick from his IV tubes, so he leaves, barricading the door of Rick's room with a gurney. Will keeping Shane alive lead to more pre-zombie flashbacks than we saw in the comic? If so, will the flashbacks, and other forms of narrative information, define Shane as a Lydia-type figure, a character whose desires are so strong that they are inexorably connected to (and represented by) a reality-shifting apocalypse? We enter the second season of the *Walking Dead* TV show in a state of thrilling uncertainty.

Currently, though, the dominant *Walking Dead* vision is Kirkman's, and it's a bleak vision, stripped of all meaning and purpose, as senseless as the moment at the end of *Night of the Living Dead* when Ben is gunned down by zombie-hunting rednecks. Why does Kirkman avoid the more desire-driven representations of apocalypse in *The Birds* and *Shaun*? We should remember that this avoidance might not be permanent: as an open-ended story, a continuing serial, the *Walking Dead* comic could introduce characters and causes responsible for the zombie plague in the very next issue. Maybe Kirkman is withholding the cause for the final issue of the comic book, or maybe he doesn't care about the cause and has nothing to reveal. Regardless, I find the unexplained, meaningless version of the zombie apocalypse presented by Romero and Kirkman scarier than the id-come-to-life metaphors of Hitchcock and Edgar Wright. In *The Birds* and *Shaun*, key characters are given subterranean power, but in Kirkman's zombieland, shit happens for no good, or bad, reason, and that may be the most frightening worldview of all.

CRAIG FISCHER is an associate professor of English at Appalachian State University. His work has appeared in *The Comics Journal*, the *International Journal of Comic*

Art, and *Transatlantica*. Fischer also regularly contributes articles on comics and comics culture to the site The Panelists (thepanelists.org) and was a judge for the 2010 Eisner Awards.

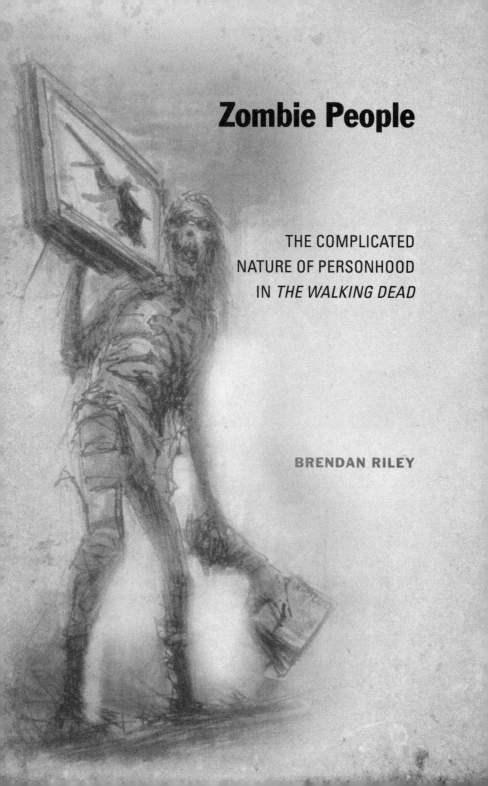

Zombie People

THE COMPLICATED
NATURE OF PERSONHOOD
IN *THE WALKING DEAD*

BRENDAN RILEY

"She's not your mother anymore."
　　　　　　　　　　—Ed, *Shaun of the Dead*

"I don't want to be walkin' around like that."
　　　　　　　　　　—Roger, *Dawn of the Dead*

"Keep your funeral, dear. Timmy and I are going zombie."
　　　　　　　　　　—Helen, *Fido*

Zombie stories scare us in many ways, triggering our primal fear of being eaten alive, our instinctive horror of corpses, and even our unconscious worry about the collapse of civilization. They spur our imagination, helping us contemplate how we would handle ourselves during a large-scale, life-threatening crisis. Most zombie tales also expose a fascinating paradox about the living dead. On one hand, the human characters believe reanimated corpses are no longer the people they once were. Nearly every zombie text features a conversation like the one from *Shaun of the Dead* (2004) in which Ed persuades Shawn that the zombie Barbara is no longer her former self. On the other hand, many stories also include a moment in which someone who has been bitten begs to be shot, as Roger does from his deathbed in *Dawn of the Dead* (1978). This paradox about the relationship between a person and their zombie corpse threads through the *Walking Dead* comic. However, because the comic has had such a long run, it takes this contradictory perspective to new extremes, challenging how we understand the relationship between minds and bodies. The comic complicates what it means to be a person and draws attention to the situated nature of our identities.

THAT'S NOT YOUR MOTHER . . . OR IS IT?

Most zombie stories assert early and often that zombies are not the people they were when they were alive. *The Walking Dead* made this perspective abundantly clear very early on. Throughout the initial story arc, "Days Gone Bye," human survivors discussed zombies only in terms of practicalities— how to kill them, how to avoid them, how they sense the world, and so on. Aside from a little initial trauma, the survivors showed no compunction about killing zombies and no concern that the zombies might be people. In "Miles Behind Us," Rick nearly came to blows with Hershel after learning that the farmer's zombified neighbors and family occupied the barn:

RICK: We're putting them out of their *misery*, and keeping them from *killing* us! Those things *aren't* human. They're undead *monsters* [. . .] I don't think I could *live* without my son . . . But you've got to listen to me, *Hershel*. That thing in the barn . . . it's *not* your son [. . .]

HERSHEL: We don't know a *goddamn thing* about them. We don't know what they're *thinking*—what they're *feeling* [. . .] For all *we* know these things could wake up *tomorrow*, heal up, and be completely *normal* again! We just don't *know*! You could have been *murdering* all those people you "put out of their misery."

The narrative up to this point provided no reason to think the zombies possess feelings or thoughts, and the events that follow bear out Rick's contention that keeping zombies around—even locked up—is dangerous: the zombies in Hershel's barn escape a few pages later, as do the zombies left alive in the unused parts of the prison. But even as Rick claimed that protecting the zombies was unreasonable, he revealed his own doubt when he used the phrase "out of their misery." Despite his uncompromising stance toward killing the zombies, he and the other survivors also recognized that the zombies might be suffering, cursed to walk the earth, always hungry.

The comic established this dynamic early on. In issue one, Rick found a zombie in the weeds next to the road. It had decayed too much to move, so it merely gasped up at Rick as he stood over it. The look on his face might have been horror or disgust, but the tear that rolled down his cheek suggested that Rick felt empathy for the pathetic creature. The end of the issue confirmed this empathy when Rick stopped on his way out of town to shoot the zombie, a moment mirrored in the first episode of the television series. Once again, he cried. The idea of empathy for the zombies appeared again in the third major story arc, "Safety Behind Bars." When Rick discovered that everyone reanimates, whether they died from a bite or not, he took a long journey to find zombie Shane. After he dug Shane up, Rick said, "When I realized you might be at the bottom of that hole, *alive*—or *whatever*—I couldn't stop *thinking* about it. I couldn't sleep—knowing you were down there. Would *you* have left *me*? [. . .] Could *you* have lived with yourself? *Not me*. I had to set things *right*." As with the zombie by the road, the fact that Rick went out of his way to put the zombie down undermines his outspoken claim that the zombies are no longer the people they once were.

More significantly, *The Walking Dead* has thus far avoided that other clichéd zombie trope: the plea to be kept from rising again. Unlike *Dawn of the Dead* (1978) or its myriad imitators, the comic implies that some people may prefer the zombie life to no life at all. Early in the series, Jim got bitten during a scuffle with some roaming zombies. As he sickened, he asked to be left alone in the woods instead of tended to (and killed) by the group, saying, "L-Leave me. When I *come back* . . . maybe I'll find—find my family . . . Maybe *they* c-came back, too. Maybe we can be together again." Despite the carnage he'd seen, Jim held out hope that being a zombie would be better than being dead. Doctor Stevens made a similar choice in the sequence "This Sorrowful Life" after being bitten. "I'm not *dying* . . . Think of it *scientifically* . . . I'm just . . . evolving . . . into a different . . . *worse* life-form. I'll still exist . . . in *some* way." Like Jim, Stevens preferred zombie life to total death. Despite claims to the contrary, the survivors continued to see the zombies, at least partly, as the people they used to be.

WHAT IS A PERSON?

Science fiction has long struggled to identify what separates people from the rest of the biosphere. Mary Shelley's *Frankenstein*, often cited as one of the first science-fiction works, turns on this very question: If we could make a creature that seemed to be a person, would that creature *be* a person? That same question has reverberated since, in works such as *2001: A Space Odyssey* (1968) and *A.I. Artificial Intelligence* (2001). When we develop the tools to create artificially intelligent entities, we will have to decide whether those creatures should have equal rights and justice under our legal system. We will need to revisit our definitions of what it means to be alive, to be sentient, and we will need to answer those individuals when they call for access to resources and opportunities to make lives of their own.

Philosophers have also considered the question of identity from a variety of different perspectives. John Locke famously claimed that consciousness defines personhood, suggesting a distinction between the mind and the body. For Locke, if two individuals were to swap minds, *Freaky Friday*–style, those minds would retain their identities in new bodies. This perspective is updated and reinforced by John Searle, whose "Chinese room" problem also differentiates between the ability to imitate consciousness and the *being* at the center of *actual* consciousness. By contrast, other philosophers find the mind inseparable from the physical brain, and work to understand how the disembodied sense of consciousness can emerge from the impulses of neurons. In *I Am a Strange Loop*, modern philosopher Douglas Hofstadter argues for a much hazier line between *person* and *non-person*, describing complexity of thought as a sliding scale on which he is unwilling to demarcate a border. Looking at the abstruse landscape of philosophy contemplating this mind/body problem, René Descartes' famous dictum, "I think, therefore I am," seems almost like an abdication from the debate.

At the same time that science-fiction writers and philosophers contemplate minds of all kinds, our political and social sciences seethe with debate over the real-world definition of personhood. It wasn't so long ago that upstanding members of society argued vigorously about whether certain human beings were, in fact, *people*. The rhetoric that classified persons of other races, faiths, or geographic heritage as subhuman served the economic and social needs of the expanding European states and America. By dehumanizing people kidnapped from Africa, for instance, Americans could rationalize treating those people like cattle (as in the Dred Scott decision, in which the U.S. Supreme Court found that slaves had no legal rights because they were property). The ongoing effects of such institutionalized racism are still visible in our culture's economic and social disparities today.

More recently, debate about personhood has focused on the beginning and end of life. At the beginning, opponents struggle to define a person in the context of a human embryo. Many pro-life advocates argue that the moment of conception should be considered the beginning of life, and that abortion should, therefore, be illegal. But pro-choice factions argue that the embryo meets none of the conditions we normally associate with life: it cannot survive outside the womb and has no clear markers like a heartbeat or brain activity. The legal system has been no help, drawing a relatively arbitrary line distinguishing "embryo" from "unborn child." Regardless of where we stand, the debate turns on how we understand *personhood*.

A similar struggle emerges over questions about when we *stop* being a person. Leaving aside thoughts on the afterlife, most everyone agrees that our personhood ends when we die. But we struggle more with changes to our state of mind. America considered this question on a national stage during the legal struggle around Terry Schiavo. In March 2005, the parents of Schiavo, a woman who had been in a persistent vegetative state (PVS) since 1990, gained national attention due to their court battle to prevent Schiavo's husband from removing her feeding tube, a process he had begun seven years earlier. The national attention amplified as members of the U.S. Congress and President Bush sided with Schiavo's parents. As the court battle progressed, debate raged about the status of people in persistent vegetative states. Some claimed PVS victims were conscious and trying to communicate by means of their damaged bodies; others argued that such communication was pareidolia, a phenomenon by which we recognize patterns in otherwise random stimuli. As with abortion, our perception of the Schiavo affair depends on when we believe someone stops being a person—if her body is alive and her brain has ceased all its higher functions, is she still alive? We can't help but wonder when she stopped being the person her family knew her to be.

We have similar concerns about individuals with less severe brain injuries. It is unclear whether significant changes to the brain via injury, disease, or medication change the person, especially if the person's behavior varies significantly because of those changes. When people with Alzheimer's, Parkinson's, or similar degenerative diseases experience dementia, they often act and speak differently. While no one would suggest that senile men and women are not *people*, many would agree that they are no longer the people they once were. The same goes for individuals with significant brain injuries. It is difficult to argue that a person with little or no memory, like Lenny in the Christopher Nolan film *Memento* (2000), is still the same person he was before his accident. People with dementia or severe brain injuries inhabit the same bodies but seem to have different minds.

On a more mundane level, the question of personhood demands a complicated answer even for people without such obvious trauma. Recovering alcoholics seem to be different people once they stop drinking. Individuals with lifelong chronic depression undergo major personality changes when they begin receiving medication to balance their brain chemistry. Both types of people see the world differently, act differently, even make and build relationships differently. We can even consider the way a person changes as he or she matures in light of this question. Few of us consider ourselves, fundamentally, to be the same person we were as a child: our outlook on the world has changed, perhaps in no lesser way than that of someone who is on a new medication or recovering from an addiction.

The Walking Dead tackles these questions throughout its long run, using the dramatic backdrop of the zombie apocalypse to bring matters of personhood and identity into stark relief. It challenges us to rethink how we understand ourselves and others.

COMPLICATED PEOPLE

Throughout *The Walking Dead*, surviving humans work very hard to define themselves in ways that maintain their sense of humanity, even at the cost of dehumanizing others. Rick and many of the other survivors tell themselves that zombies are no longer people, as if intentionally avoiding their suspicions that the undead are more complicated than that. To be fair, the world of the comic demands such a perspective. Hershel's pained pleas for his zombified son, Shawn, to "remember!" fell on necrotic ears, just as Tyreese's cries did nothing to tame his daughter Julie after she turned at the prison in "Safety Behind Bars." The unrelenting horror of being eaten by their loved ones pushed the survivors to pretend they have an uncompromising attitude toward the zombies.

At the same time, in moments of calm, some members of the group took a more nuanced view of the zombies. For instance, while he and Hershel plowed the prison yard for crops, Axel mused about the zombies:

> I think about them all the time. Who they *were*—what they did before they *died*—all kinds of stuff [. . .] I wonder what it felt like when they died. I wonder what it was like to start turning

into one of them—to come *back*. I wonder if it *hurts*. I *bet* it
hurts real bad. That's why they moan so much. You gotta ask
yourselves these questions. ("The Heart's Desire")

During this conversation, which Hershel frowned on, Axel
underscored the similarities between people and zombies. He
read emotion in their actions and empathized with them. Sophia
and Carl expressed similar thoughts a few pages earlier. When
Carl asked Sophia why she felt sorry for the zombies, she said,
"Because they look so sad. Don't they look *sad* to you?" When
the survivors are not in fight-or-flight mode, they have time to
reflect on their close relationship to the zombies, which softens
their hardened stance toward the walking dead.

Conversely, in times of trouble, the humans applied the same
dehumanizing strategies to one another that they used to maintain the line between humans and zombies. This became most
evident in the Woodbury story arc. Rick, Glenn, and Michonne
discovered a neighboring community of survivors ruled by a
madman called the Governor. While the narrative focused mostly
on the Governor and his villainous henchmen, it also provided a
clear sense that the people living in Woodbury did not realize the
extent of the Governor's horrific crimes. In fact, his political savvy
allowed him to paint Rick and the other survivors in the prison
as vicious enemies. Later, after he recovered from Michonne's
attack, the Governor gave a speech calling Rick's group "ruthless,
inhuman savages" and "monsters." During the following attack,
his people believed they were fighting for a just cause against
murderers. While the comic clearly established the Governor as
a madman, the speech mentioned above sounds familiar because
Rick used it not too much earlier. After discovering that Martinez
intended to lead the Woodbury group to the prison, Rick ran him
down with the RV and throttled him as he lay on the ground.

Shouting at the dying man, Rick used the same rhetoric: "*You people* are a *poison*—a plague *worse* than the *dead*! [. . .] *You're animals*!" While strangling Martinez to death, Rick shouted, "*Don't you know what people are capable of*?!"

This parallel language highlights the ease with which humans in the story twisted their own priorities to survive. At times, *The Walking Dead* blurs the line between human and inhuman, calling into question values by which the characters (and, vicariously, the audience) define humanity. This becomes all the more clear in the regular similarity between images of people and of zombies throughout the comic. For example, near the beginning of "The Heart's Desire," the humans battled a herd of zombies inside the prison fence. Adlard rendered eight humans and eight zombies in a grid of sixteen portraits, with each featuring varying amounts of chiaroscuro, explosions or wounds, and open, angry mouths. The mix of images created a graphic parallel between the zombies and the humans: at a quick glance, the two groups appear quite similar. The cover art of various editions of the comic also bears out this parallel. Most strikingly, the cover of the first *The Walking Dead Compendium* features a mirrored image with the humans on the top and zombie versions of the characters below.

At the same time, as the humans used language to keep themselves from seeing zombies as people and to see antagonistic survivors as less than people, the comic presents anomalies that prod the reader to doubt that the line between zombie and human is as clear as Rick's group claims. Most striking are the zombies who were traveling with Michonne when she first arrived at the prison. She kept them in chains and had removed their lower jaws; they walked along behind her, apparently keeping other zombies at bay. When Otis asked about them, she said, "These two stopped trying to attack me a *long* time ago. My boyfriend and his best friend." Up to that point in the comic, there had not been any other "tame" zombies. Later, in the story arc "The Best Defense," we learned a bit more about zombie psychology from the Governor, who revealed that well-fed zombies are happier and less likely to attack. We also discovered that the Governor was keeping his zombified daughter chained up in his apartment. These developments complicate the notion that zombies are empty shells operating on the hunger instinct alone. Instead, they can be sated and even trained.

Finally, *The Walking Dead* seethes with the question that has haunted us as long as we've had civilizations: What happens to our humanity when we do inhumane things? Our first glimpse of the coming turbulence arose toward the end of "Days Gone Bye," when Carl shot Shane to defend Rick. Clinging tightly to Rick, Carl sobbed, "It's not the same as killing the *dead* ones, Daddy." Rick held him close and answered, "It never *should* be, Son." Rick's answer serves as an anthem throughout the comic, providing a bearing when he lamented that he had drifted too far away from the man he believed himself to be. For example, after he killed Martinez in "This Sorrowful Life," Rick worried that he had lost his moral center:

> Killing him made me *realize* something—made me *notice* how much I've changed. I used to be a trained police officer—my job was to *uphold* the *law*. Now I feel more like a lawless *savage*—an *animal*. I *killed* a man today and I don't even *care* [. . .] But it made me realize how *detached* I've become. I'd kill *every single one* of the people here if I thought it'd keep you safe [. . .] Does that make me *evil*?

The desensitizing effect of killing so many undead and the violence all around him shook Rick's ideas about who he is.

Despite his own sense that his actions were correct, Rick suggested that he had changed, and worried that he had violated the code he'd sworn to uphold when he became a police officer.

INHUMANE HUMANS

Throughout the comic we see many instances of people whose actions in the wake of the zombie apocalypse fundamentally changed who they were. "Fear the Hunters" illustrates these changes particularly well, underlining the notion that one's actions define one's humanity, or lack thereof.

First, the group had to grapple with Ben, the boy who killed his brother for apparently no reason at all. Early in the series, the boys seemed relatively normal, but over the course of the first nine volumes, they lost both their parents and saw friends murdered. Violence was a part of their daily lives for as long as they could remember. While the readers got an early glimpse of Ben's emerging madness when we saw him vivisecting a cat at the end of "What We Become," his brother's murder came as a shock to the survivors. Ben's act fundamentally changed him in their eyes. They realized that he really didn't grasp the difference between right and wrong; as Michonne put it, "He's a boy who doesn't understand *murder*." But they also wrestled with what do to about him. Abraham summarized their dilemma:

> If this kind of thing happened in the real world—before all this madness—he'd get what—*twenty years* of therapy? He'd be sent off to some kind of home for the rest of his life and even then they'd probably *never* fix him. That's not an option here. None of us are therapists . . . none of us can help this boy. He's simply a burden—a *liability*.

Therapy is a luxury in their world, and they don't have the resources to handle a dangerous person among them. Like Thomas, the serial killer in "Safety Behind Bars," the only solution seems to be to kill the murderer. Unlike the situation with Thomas, however, the adults in the group are hampered by their affection for Ben and are hesitant to kill a child.

The last panel on the page exploring this debate shows that Carl, another child who has grown up over the course of the comic, has no such hesitation—his determined scowl makes it quite clear that he understands what needs to be done. While the adults still wrestle with their allegiance to the "real world" they grew up in, Carl grasps the more vicious but necessary law of survival at work throughout the comic. Thus he kills Ben in the night before Ben can kill again. When Carl and his father later talk about it, Rick reiterates that, "When we do these things and we're good people . . . they're still *bad* things. You can never lose sight of that. If these things start becoming *easy*, that's when it's all over. That's when we become bad people." Rick, Carl, Abraham, and the others struggle daily to understand how the context of someone's actions defines their humanity. Ben's senseless and remorseless murder of his brother made him monstrous; Carl's hesitant but moral killing keeps him sympathetic.

Then the group met Father Stokes, a priest whose own sense of self had been sorely tested since he locked himself in his church and left his congregation outside to die. When Rick and the other survivors met him, he was wracked with guilt over his inaction, and had not yet really had to defend himself against zombies or other people. After Dale disappeared, Rick confronted Father Stokes, who confessed his cowardice. Stokes sobbed, "I know what I did. I know what I *deserve*. Kill me. Please. I've suffered enough—I *want* you to do it." Then he collapsed in a corner, weeping. Father Stokes' actions highlight another kind of moral lapse: his failure to protect those around him.

Up to this point, the failure to act had not been a strong storyline in *The Walking Dead*. One could argue that Hershel the farmer suffered from this problem, as did some of the side characters in Woodbury who failed to intervene against the Governor, but these storylines were incidental to the main focus on the way murder and killing erode one's humanity. By contrast, the Father Stokes storyline highlights how someone could become monstrous by failing to follow through with his ideals. When Stokes locked the doors to his church and left his congregation outside to die, he failed to uphold his principles. His dead parishioners haunted him, leading him to beg Rick to end his life. Father Stokes' selfishness represents a different kind of inhumanity brought forth by crisis.

Finally, the suburban cannibals presented another inhuman perspective with which Rick and his friends grappled in "Fear the Hunters." As the survivors mourned the deaths of Billy and Ben, Dale was captured by a cadre of hunters who preyed on passing groups. When Rick confronted them, they explained that cannibalism was their last recourse and that they had eaten not only people who happened by, but even their own children. The survivors overpowered the cannibals, then tortured them. As Rick described it later:

> I can't stop thinking about what we did to the hunters. I know it's justifiable . . . but I see them when I close my eyes . . . Doing what we did, to living people . . . after taking their weapons . . . it *haunts* me. I see every bloody bit. Every broken bone. Every bashed in skull. They did what they did, but we *mutilated* those people. Made the others watch as we went through them . . . one by one.

Rick continued to be haunted by the actions he and others had taken to survive, but the things they were willing to do kept getting more vicious. Rick's claim to be justified in torturing the cannibals stretches beyond the ethical framework he had clung to so far: even savage actions are acceptable in order to protect the group, but that savagery must be tempered by necessity, and the living must recognize it as "bad." Torturing the hunters may have crossed that line.

The ethical and emotional trials facing the survivors in "Fear the Hunters" highlight the many ways times of crisis challenge the ideals on which we base our humanity. When Ben killed Billy, the group had to reconsider its approach to justice in order to weigh the responsibility of a child murderer against the safety of the group. The Father Stokes storyline introduced the idea that inaction could be just as immoral as action. And in torturing the hunters, Rick and the other survivors further undermined their own hold on civilization, killing not for self-defense, but for punishment as well.

WE ARE THE WALKING DEAD

At the end of "The Heart's Desire," Rick stomped around the prison yard, yelling at the other survivors. He blamed himself for being naïve and shouted that they were becoming the very dead they'd sought to kill. He claimed that they would still try to know right from wrong, but that they would do whatever it took to survive. Then, in a bleak moment of despair, he raged, "We *are* the walking dead!"

The complicated nature of personhood in *The Walking Dead* undermined the black-and-white moral judgments Rick had been trying to make. Throughout the series, survivors contrast their humanity with the savagery of others, often finding the values they attached to being human challenged by the circumstances of their survival. When Tyreese objected that they "don't *want* to become *savages*," Rick replied, "We *already are* savages." In doing whatever it took to survive, Rick and the others had fundamentally changed their own natures. But at the same time, Rick consistently returned to the idea of conscience as the key to maintaining one's humanity, relying on his ability to recognize acts as "bad but necessary" to reassure himself that he was still a good person.

The violent circumstances facing characters in *The Walking Dead* force them to make choices that are far more extreme than anything most of us will ever experience. But just as Rick finds the values he holds most dear challenged by the difficult decisions he must make, so too must we struggle with challenges facing our own civilization. From the fractious line between technology and ethics to the give-and-take between individual liberty and collective need, the choices we make force us to weigh circumstances against values. In the darkest times, perhaps we're not so different from Rick, in that the best we can do is to cling to the values we hold most dear, so that we can remain good people, even when we must do bad things.

BRENDAN RILEY is an associate professor of English at Columbia College Chicago, where he has been teaching, among other things, a January-session course called "Zombies in Popular Media" since 2007. He has published essays on detectives, comics, writing, and monster movies, and will likely fare poorly in the zombie apocalypse. Online at curragh-labs.org.

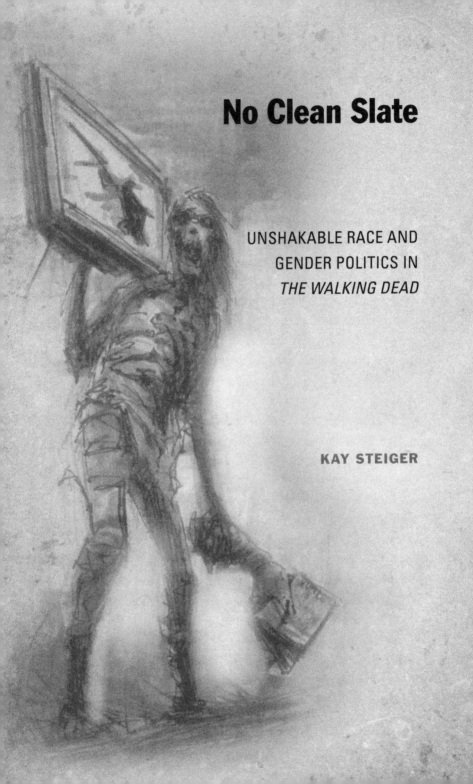

No Clean Slate

UNSHAKABLE RACE AND GENDER POLITICS IN *THE WALKING DEAD*

KAY STEIGER

The *Walking Dead* comic, created by Robert Kirkman, Tony Moore, and Charlie Adlard, and the television adaptation, produced by Frank Darabont, have been critically acclaimed, and the show set a record as "the most watched drama series in basic cable history," according to the *New York Times*. But some feminist critics and antiracist bloggers haven't so lovingly embraced the show. They argue that *The Walking Dead*, for all its adoring praise, falls into some sadly familiar traps with its poor depictions of women and people of color. *The Walking Dead*'s portrayal of race issues and gender roles has been, by far, the most controversial aspect of the series.

Sites such as Feministing, Feministe, Racialicious, and Geek Feminism have gained popularity in recent years. They critique popular culture and identify sexism and racism as means of teaching its prevention. They have become the noisy concerned citizens groups of the internet, crying out when they see injustice in the media. These bloggers have analyzed *The Walking Dead* with the same vigor they have other pieces of popular culture. And they have a long list of things to complain about.

It's hard to miss the racial tension in *The Walking Dead*, especially in the television adaptation. In the second episode of the series ("Guts"), Merle Dixon hurls racial slurs at T-Dog, a black member of the survival group, while they scavenge for supplies in Atlanta. Merle's racist rants are inopportune and straightforwardly put the group at risk.

Scott Meslow, in an episode recap on the *Atlantic*'s website, finds the actions of Merle Dixon "barely coherent." He argues one way to read this scene: that Merle seems to have bafflingly decided "a zombie attack that literally requires cooperation for survival is the right time to alienate everyone." But Cyriaque Lamar offers in an episode recap for io9, a pop culture blog, another way to read this: "We ... learned that being a crazy white supremacist is an old habit that dies hard." Indeed, though many of the show's critics object to some of the race and gender issues presented, a common theme in the series itself seems to be that a postapocalyptic zombie world is no clean slate when it comes to these issues.

Neither Merle nor his equally racist brother, Daryl, who is introduced in the third episode ("Tell It to the Frogs"), appear in the *Walking Dead* comics. Their insertion into the television adaptation has been cited as odd and awkward by many bloggers. Shani Hilton, who writes for the racial justice website Colorlines, comments in her personal blog that the racism depicted in the television show is "cartoonish." The addition of the Dixons could have been done for a couple of reasons. First, simply and straightforwardly, to create dramatic tension. Race bloggers often find such sprinkling of racial tension as a substitution for dramatic tension to be lazy and reductive—racist characters are often a cue for readers or viewers that these people are purely "bad," when, in fact, racism in life is far more complex and sometimes comes from the "good guys."

Though the television show caught flak for adding racial tension and stereotypes to the series, racial issues aren't absent from the comic books. In volume four, "The Heart's Desire," subtler elements of racial tension emerge.

Michonne, a black female character who displays some serious sword-wielding skills, aggressively seduces Tyreese, another black character, who is developed as one of the survival group's leaders along with central protagonist Rick Grimes. Up to that point, Tyreese had been romantically involved with a white character, Carol, who ultimately slits her wrists after witnessing Michonne's advances and Tyreese's reception of them. The assertive nature of Michonne's appeal to Tyreese comes across to some as steeped in pre–civil rights stereotypes of hypersexual black people. In fact, since Carol ultimately turns suicidal, one interpretation of this could be that black sexuality is so powerful that it is threatening to white people.

The Governor, a villainous white man who first appears in volume six, "This Sorrowful Life," could come under criticism for a lack of character complexity since he is so clearly depicted as pure evil: he and his followers engage in cannibalism, he keeps his zombie daughter chained to a wall, and he rapes and tortures Michonne. It is this last scene that has elicited much criticism from antiracist readers and bloggers, who say the rape is depicted in a graphic, even sexualized, way.

Because *The Walking Dead* depicts a white man raping a black woman, it conjures up a dark period in American history. In Danielle McGuire's 2010 book, *At the End of the Dark Street: Black Women, Rape, and Resistance—A New History of the Civil Rights Movement from Rosa Parks to the Rise of Black Power*, she documents a time in the pre–civil rights South, when "former slaveholders and their sympathizers used rape as a 'weapon of terror' to dominate the bodies and minds of African-American men and women." Prominent civil rights activist Rosa Parks was a leader in attempting to prosecute the men who perpetrated these crimes against black women. The scene that depicts Michonne's rape reflects that time of terror. Though perhaps Kirkman intended to drive home the point that the Governor is evil through this scene, it is troubling because it ends up reinforcing a historical reality that still hasn't been fully acknowledged or reconciled.

It should be noted that some depictions of race relations in the *Walking Dead* comics are positive. Interracial friendships and romantic relationships are portrayed as completely normal. And they should be. A 2007 Gallup poll shows that a majority of Americans support interracial marriage. A more detailed Pew study, released in 2010, shows that 63 percent of Americans support interracial relationships in all circumstances and that 80 percent of Americans approve of interracial marriages with at least one other race. In addition to the relationship between Tyreese and Carol (which, admittedly, ends badly), the comic books portray an interracial relationship between Julie and Chris, as well as one between Glenn and Maggie. These may not be enough to make up for the negative race depictions that, intentionally or not, reinforce negative ideas about race, but they show that Kirkman realizes that issues surrounding race are complex.

Just as antiracist bloggers take issue with some aspects of *The Walking Dead*, feminist bloggers also weigh in. Jennifer Smith writes in the blog Fantastic Fangirls, "One of the biggest concerns for me with *The Walking Dead* has been the troubling gender issues [. . .] The problem comes up when issues of gender inequality are present, questioned within the text, and then summarily dismissed." Smith cites characters that find male-dominated leadership of the group unobjectionable, pointing to a scene in volume one, "Days Gone Bye," when the tasks are designated along traditional gender lines. "One female character is frustrated by this stereotypical division of labor and wonders, when the zombies are gone, if women will even be allowed to vote. But the other women in the scene laugh off her fears. They know nothing about guns, after all, and shouldn't they do what they're good at? The characters continue doing laundry, the matter settled."

Yan Basque writes for the blog Irrelevant Comics, "Kirkman seems to think that men and women are fundamentally different in ways that go beyond the physical/anatomical [. . .] There are of course a few exceptions. [Andrea] is a good shooter, while Tyreese can't shoot to save his life. But these are just that: exceptions." Clearly, Kirkman didn't make many friends in the girl geek blogosphere with some of his choices.

Feminist critiques have recently gained more traction in mainstream media. Tad Friend writes in an April 2011 *New Yorker* profile of actress Anna Faris about the Bechdel test, a simple method to determine if a piece of popular culture exhibits gender bias. This test has become the standard by which feminist critics judge television, movies, books, and other media. For a work to pass the test—for it to have realistic female characters—the story must have at least two women in it, they must talk to each other, and they must talk about something other than a man. Friend's profile marks the first time *The New Yorker* mentioned this test, despite the fact that it was first developed in a comic strip by cartoonist Alison Bechdel in 1985. Feminist critics have long used the test to discuss popular culture, but its appearance in a literary magazine like *The New Yorker* marks its entrance into mainstream criticism.

Applying this standard to the *Walking Dead*'s television pilot on AMC, Courtney Stoker writes on the blog Geek Feminism, "This episode failed the Bechdel test *hard*, despite being an hour and a half long, and a fucking zombie movie, not a rom com" (emphasis in original). Feminist critics have no shortage of things to complain about in the universe of *The Walking Dead*, in both the TV series and the comics.

Characters exhibit behavior based on traditional gender roles—this comes off as strange in a world where the top priority is survival. When the group arrives at the prison complex near the end of volume two, "Miles Behind Us," for instance, it is the first time they begin to feel safe from the roamers for an extended period. But it is also when the women take up traditional household chores, making new clothing for the group out of sheets and prison uniforms. Carol laments the lack of domestic work in a scene with Lori. "What we need are some knitting needles," she says. Feminism and domestic activities such as knitting certainly aren't mutually exclusive, but given that *The Walking Dead* portrays a world in which survival is so important, it's downright strange that Carol misses crafty domestic pastimes while her family lives in a jail cell and zombies storm the gates.

Later, after Carol feels rejected by Tyreese, near the end of volume four and into volume five, "The Best Defense," she tries to initiate a plural marriage with Rick and Lori, which seems to suggest that Carol feels lost. Though a plural marriage doesn't seem traditional, it's clear that Carol is desperate to cling to Lori and Rick, who she views as fulfilling a more traditional gender dynamic. Rick's role as a traditional male leader and Lori's role as a mother and caretaker are comforting to Carol.

Indeed, the conversations more generally among women in the group often turn to domestic matters: What should the group eat? What should they do to pass the time? What are the challenges of caring for the children in this environment? The men, on the other hand, converse about long-term survival: gathering supplies, group organization, and protection. It is precisely this kind of categorical division of gender roles that Smith, Basque, and Stoker find so objectionable. Frustratingly, some of the worst gender dynamics in today's world are replicated in the ones with murderous zombies.

A major example of the difference between men's and women's roles is demonstrated by a collective choice about the group's leadership structure. Rick emerges as the leader early on in the comic series, taking over once Shane dies, but after they arrive at the prison, things change. A confrontation between Rick and another leader of the group, Tyreese, ends in a violent brawl. While Rick recovers from his wounds, Dale informs him that he is no longer the sole leader. Dale tells Rick that the group voted that the two of them, plus Hershel and Tyreese, will form a committee to make decisions on everyone's behalf. Rick, thinking this choice seems strange, asks, "The four of us? Really? No women?"

Dale explains that the women declined leadership: "They're fine with *us* making the decisions [. . .] I think they just want to be protected." Andrea and Michonne, who play more important protective roles than the other women in the group, have said they don't want to take on leadership, even when pressed by the others.

There are several ways to interpret this scene. It could be that Kirkman is relying on old stereotypes and genuinely believes that women naturally defer to men when it comes to making decisions. This is an idea that—uncomfortable as it is for most women to admit—is reflected in real life: a survey conducted in early 2011 by MassMutual Financial Group found that women express much less confidence in investment decisions than men do. Though the circumstances of the MassMutual survey are less apocalyptic than the ones in *The Walking Dead*, there seems to be some indication that, for whatever reason, there are certain decisions in life that women tend to feel less confident making.

A less positive interpretation would be that Kirkman is, consciously or unconsciously, buying into the stereotype of women as incapable of leadership during a crisis. Or, perhaps, he is aware of the old notion of men as better decision makers and is commenting on this perception with this scene. Kirkman might be presenting the women's choice to give up power as a commentary on how people rely on stereotypes in times of crisis—they are a crutch that people cling to, for better or worse.

This last seems to be the reading supported by the text itself, since Kirkman does not put the male leadership group forward as infallible or even entirely competent. They don't always make the best decisions. An investigation into the nearby town of Woodbury puts members of their group at risk, and leads to the torture of some members of the group at the hands of the Governor. This eventually causes the group to decide to leave the prison and strike out once again into the world filled with homicidal undead.

Still, feminist critics like Smith point to the leadership committee scene in particular as an egregious violation of what a feminist story in a world of zombies would look like. In theory, the zombie apocalypse is the ultimate meritocracy, a do-over for humanity in which survival skills—whether they belong to men or women—top other traits such as race, gender, and class. Intentionally or not, what Kirkman reveals with scenes like this is that stereotypes about race and gender will pop up again, even when there are no longer social structures to keep them in place.

The television series depicts a scene of traditional gender roles that would have been right at home in a John Ford Western; episode three shows the women doing the camp laundry while the men return to Atlanta for supplies. The depictions of laundry as the women's job aren't exclusive to the television series, however. The comic book also shows scenes of female characters doing laundry in washing machines once they arrive at the prison. This scene is unsettlingly, perhaps even distastefully, retro. There are few people in the survivor group to do vital everyday tasks, so it seems a huge waste to assign all the women the menial domestic work.

But the laundry scene in the television series isn't totally wretched from a feminist perspective. This scene passes the Bechdel test. Here, women talk freely to one another about issues that other women understand, like missing one's vibrator in a world without electricity. The scene reveals a kind of sister-hood salon that allows women a sanctuary in the midst of what has suddenly become for them a very hard life.

There are other examples of women breaking gender bar-riers—as Basque notes, exceptions—and important ones at that. The creators of *The Walking Dead* give vitally important gun and sword skills to two female characters in a world in which such skills are needed most—a move that flies in the face of many stereotypes of women in postapocalyptic fiction. Normally, it is women who need saving and men who do it.

The two very strong female characters in *The Walking Dead* are Andrea, a sharpshooter, and Michonne, who impresses the survivor group with her deadly sword skills. Andrea and Michonne have much in common, but they aren't friends. They rarely interact, and when they do, it's tense. In volume four, "The Heart's Desire," Andrea happens upon Michonne in the middle of an imaginary conversation with her dead boyfriend. When Andrea asks her about the conversation, inquiring whether she's all right, Michonne denies that she was doing anything out of the ordinary. After an uncomfortable pause, Andrea mutters "fucking *bitch*" under her breath.

This distrust and skepticism between strong female characters highlights another facet of gender roles of concern to feminist critics. In many ways, it is the dark side of the Bechdel test. If women talk to one another about something other than a man but do so only in the context of confronting or competing with one another, is that really progress?

This tension between strong female characters in a group dominated by men is a fairly common trope in pop culture. Scenes in the AMC drama *Mad Men* explore this idea by depicting contentious conversations between Christina Hendricks' character, Joan, and Elisabeth Moss' character, Peggy, who each hold a different kind of power in a man's world. Brilliant comedienne Tina Fey also explores this idea in her critically acclaimed NBC comedy *30 Rock* with an episode titled "TGS Hates Women." The episode illustrates the difficulty women often feel they face in the workplace: Fey's character, Liz Lemon, oscillates between wanting to mentor a younger woman because they have so much in common and disliking the attention she seems to get from their male colleagues.

Such stereotypes manifest themselves in real life, too. Julianna Margulies responded to industry executives who said her show, *The Good Wife*, would be fighting for ratings against Dana Delany's *Body of Proof*. "It's like, of course, you finally have two great female leads and you're going to put us on against each other," she said in a May 2011 interview with *The Huffington Post*. "You're assholes."

Andrea is portrayed largely as a strong character, but her strength is challenged later in the series, when the group enters the Alexandria Safe-Zone in volume twelve of *The Walking Dead*, "Life Among Them." There she encounters the lecherous Douglas Monroe, former U.S. congressman and guardian of the Alexandria Safe-Zone. He sets his sights on Andrea, who says she isn't interested in pursuing a romantic encounter with a married man. Still, Andrea is deprived of her power in this scene. To Monroe, the only value she has is as a sexual object. Likewise,

Michonne, in the rape scene with the Governor, has her power and agency as a strong woman stripped away by male power.

But if gender stereotypes can be bad for women in *The Walking Dead*, then they most certainly can be for men, too. In his personal blog, libertarian writer Will Wilkerson identifies some of the issues men have with feminism and pushes for gender equality: "Men aren't angry and confused because they don't know what women want. They're angry because they want what their fathers or grandfathers had and they can't get it. They're confused because they can't quite grasp why not."

In many ways, this is a perspective that Shane represents, especially in the television iteration of his character. At the beginning of the pilot episode, Shane, Rick's friend and fellow officer, spouts a prolonged rant against women as he and Rick sit in the patrol car eating burgers and fries. Shane tells Rick that he has "never met a woman who knew how to turn off a light."

Then, Shane launches into a long rant, calling himself "Reverend Shane" who preaches from the "Guy Gospel." Many women, such as Jennifer Smith at Fantastic Fangirls, object to this clearly sexist rant. Shane's character in this scene is reinforcing the ideas that he is exhibiting superiority over women. It's clearly ridiculous to claim all women can't turn off lights when they leave the room—even Rick says he doesn't have that problem with Lori. Shane is marking himself as someone who has generally low opinions of women.

Later, when the group arrives at the Centers for Disease Control building at the end of season one, Shane corners Lori in the library and attempts to sexually assault her. In the comic book, Shane's struggle with masculinity is subtler. Shane starts out as Lori's savior, lover, and likely the father of her second child, but he feels threatened when Rick returns. In volume one, "Days Gone Bye," Shane seems jealous of Rick's life. When the world falls apart and he and Lori both think Rick is dead, Shane can finally have that life. But after Rick's return, his attitude takes a darker turn, seemingly because the life he thought he had is gone. Shane considers killing Rick and is shot by Carl when he threatens to carry out his plan.

Taken together, these different iterations of Shane add up to what Wilkerson talks about: Shane's attitude is one of entitlement. He sees Lori as an object, something to be possessed, but Lori—both in the comics and the television show—doesn't go along with Shane's plan. In both situations, he becomes violent. He can't figure out how to get what he wants, so he takes it.

In the television adaptation, it isn't just Shane who feels threatened by women. In the laundry scene, Andrea admits to the other women that what she misses the most is her vibrator. The women break into laughter after Carol whispers, "Me, too." The laughter causes Ed, Carol's husband, to investigate. He orders the women to stop laughing and stick to doing the laundry. "Don't think I won't knock you on your ass," Ed tells Andrea when she stands up to him. In the resulting scuffle, Ed slaps Carol. Ed seeks to control his wife, behavior that is common among abusers. His assault of Carol breaks the spell of the sisterly gabbing.

Shane then attacks Ed to protect the women, but he loses control while fighting him, continuing to beat him after Ed clearly gives up. Carol apologizes to Ed and tends to his wounds. (In the comic, Carol references the fact that Ed, who is already dead, once abused her, but because Carol is mentally unstable, it is unclear what her relationship with Ed was actually like.) Domestic violence, like racism and sexism, doesn't go away when zombies take over.

Carol's groveling for forgiveness in the aftermath of Shane's beating is an uncomfortable moment for viewers. She's desperate to hang on to Ed despite the fact that he mistreats her.

The National Coalition Against Domestic Violence outlines the major reasons that women stay with abusers: a lack of outside resources, outside pressure to stay and "make it work," and traditional societal pressures that reinforce the idea that men naturally tend toward violence. Abused women often find it difficult to leave, sometimes resorting to desperate measures to get out of an abusive situation: PBS reported that the FBI estimates 1,500 deaths each year are from partners killing their abusers. While a cringe-worthy moment for viewers, Carol's situation in *The Walking Dead* is reflective of real life.

For all the objections to the depictions of race and gender in *The Walking Dead*, these critics, to some degree, are missing the point. Racism and sexism exhibit themselves every day in a world without a zombie apocalypse; we shouldn't expect these problems to disappear when humans are fighting for their very survival. An exploration of questions of racism and sexism is as valid as the exploration of questions of morality that is common in postapocalyptic fiction. For example, in volume three, "Safety Behind Bars," the group enters the prison—a seeming safe haven—only to discover that one of the men there, Thomas, is a murderer, but not before he beheads Rachel and Susie Greene and threatens Andrea with a knife. After the group learns that Thomas is the killer, Rick severely beats him. The group is faced with the moral question of whether to kill a murderer. Such a dramatic situation, especially when set in a fantastic world, allows writers to freely explore what constraints keep humans from killing or mistreating one another. Similarly, writers are free to explore whether racism and sexism exhibit themselves because of civilization or in spite of it.

Much like the world in which we live now, the postapocalyptic zombie world of *The Walking Dead* isn't always good for women. Women are portrayed as victims of sexual assault, trapped in situations of domestic violence, and subject to stereo-typical attitudes about gender roles. Likewise, racism doesn't disappear the minute zombies arrive on the scene: characters like Merle Dixon still fling racist remarks at T-Dog, black people are still stereotyped as hypersexual, and interracial sexual violence still exists.

These scenarios stem from the same old racial and gender stereotypes that have existed (and that have been driving femi-nists and civil rights activists crazy) for decades. But an alternate way to interpret these depictions is that the creators are aware of what they're doing—they're not just sprinkling racism and sexism into *The Walking Dead* by accident or because they're biased themselves; depicting sexism or racism is not the same as endorsing it. Kirkman and the writers of *The Walking Dead* TV series could be choosing to put these aspects of life into their works because these problems are real. Zombies won't change that.

In theory, the greatest danger in *The Walking Dead* should be the undead or whatever caused the zombie plague in the first place. In actuality, it is humans that must be feared the most. Some of the worst threats in the series—rape, domestic violence, murder, sexism, and racism—are all issues that exist in the world today. If anything, the presence of the living dead only makes those threats more likely, not less.

KAY STEIGER is the online managing editor of *Washing-tonian* magazine. She graduated from the University of Minnesota and currently lives in Washington, D.C. She writes about reproductive justice, higher education, and popular culture. Her work has been highlighted in *The*

Atlantic, Bitch Magazine, AlterNet, Religion Dispatches, In These Times, The American Prospect, and others. She has also contributed to *Feministe, Jezebel,* and *Think Progress.* Online at kaysteiger.wordpress.com or follow Kay on Twitter @kaysteiger.

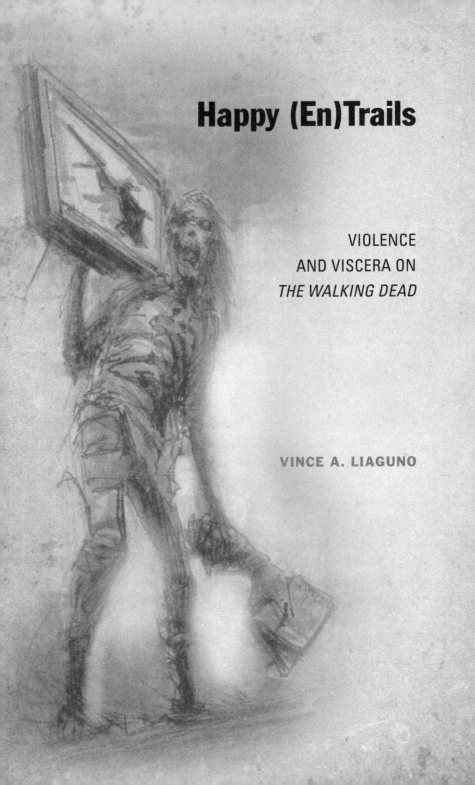

Happy (En)Trails

VIOLENCE AND VISCERA ON *THE WALKING DEAD*

VINCE A. LIAGUNO

Half a dozen or so people are gathered around a campfire under the starry night sky. There are stories being whispered in low voices, hot coffee being sipped, and marshmallows being roasted. A fresh-faced college-bound blonde named Amy, on the eve of her birthday, emerges from a nearby camper expressing to the group her disbelief that they're out of toilet paper. By all measures, the scene is unremarkable, eminently familiar. A typical group of family and friends on a camping trip to the casual observer.

Then, in a nanosecond fused with sudden movement and a low, aggressive moan, a zombie enters stage right and grabs the girl's arm, sinking its teeth hungrily into her flesh. A graphic spray of blood whips across our television screen.

AMC's series *The Walking Dead* has made healthy, unapologetic use of gore, with intestines spilling out of torsos like candy from a piñata, strips of flesh being peeled from the faces of screaming victims like banana skins, and limbs being torn from bodies with gleeful abandon. The show's special makeup effects—courtesy of Greg Nicotero and company—are a lavish buffet of the macabre, gruesome to the eye of the casual beholder and impressive to even those of us who've already journeyed through a zombie apocalypse or two.

All the more remarkable, then, that the predominant bloodletting on *The Walking Dead*—a given on a show about the flesh-eating undead—really takes a backseat to . . . wait for it . . . character and storytelling. And perhaps it's the show's uncanny ability to seamlessly integrate graphic violence into the fabric of its apocalyptic tapestry that gives *The Walking Dead* its real cultural significance.

Face it: heads being blown apart in lifelike detail is hardly standard Sunday night TV fare. In fact, it's about as far from the fuzzy family funnies of *AFV* or the haute couture catfighting campiness of *Desperate Housewives* as one could travel in the entertainment spectrum. Yet it's the characters' struggle to adhere to quickly vanishing social decorum that relegates the splattering brains to visual background noise. Viewers are so rapt as the cross section of survivors face the reality of the new societal paradigm brought on by the apocalypse that dismembered limbs and haphazardly discarded innards are but minor bloody details. This is, in no small part, testament to the superior storytelling skills of series producer Frank Darabont and the show's first-season writers, who managed to make one of television's most violent shows as legitimate a water cooler drama as cable's other infamously ultra-violent show, *The Sopranos*, once was. With 5.3 million viewers tuning into the series premiere, and coverage in major media outlets such as *Time* and *The Wall Street Journal*, *The Walking Dead* has come crashing out of the TV gates. Not satisfied to be consigned to the usual genre niche—a few lavish pages in *Fangoria* or a spot center stage for the fans at Comic-Con—*The Walking Dead* has invaded mainstream America much like the zombie outbreak of its fictional landscape. And it's captured that mass-market attention while showcasing some spectacularly grim and gory content.

Take, for example, the end of the show's first episode, during which protagonist Rick Grimes is thrown from his horse in the middle of a zombie mêlée on the streets of downtown Atlanta. A horde of hungry undead quickly attack the hapless stallion.

It's a graphic scene; an army of arms reach into a cavernous hole that's been ripped into the animal's side and pull out seemingly endless yards of bloody entrails and chunks of fleshy organs. The audience is fittingly horrified by the defenseless animal's frantic braying and kicking hooves as its innards are torn from its equestrian flanks. Then the camera pulls back to an aerial view as zombies overrun the tank in which Grimes has taken refuge. The undead scurry over and around the tank like ants on a discarded M&M at a picnic. It's this bleak scene that gets people buzzing in internet chat rooms and across social media sites.

Grimes' fate seems all but sealed, and the grim ending baffles us as audience members with its sheer hopelessness. Could the writers be so audacious as to have tricked us into believing this ordinary small-town cop was to be our lead character, our hero even, only to kill him off so quickly? The possibility lingers because, with the slaughter of the horse moments earlier, *The Walking Dead* has just broken the second of two generally accepted cultural taboos in modern entertainment—no killing of animals or children. Of course the show opens with the assassination of a child-shaped thing, too, as Rick shoots the bunny slipper-clad zombie kid that menaces him. So within the confines of its first two hours, the writers have let us know quite clearly that our expectations can and will be dashed, a fact we need to remember as we ponder Grimes' chance of escaping the seemingly inescapable situation in which he has been placed.

That, ladies and gentlemen, qualifies as superior storytelling, at least in this pop culturist's book.

As for the violence being flashed across all those millions of screens around the world, it is shocking. Appendages and internal organs being forcibly ripped from bodies surely qualifies as extremely violent under any circumstances, set in any era—past, present, or future—by definition alone. But the gore and gruesomeness has not caused a massive outcry, certainly nothing like the panic spawned by far less startling television violence in the past.

Public indignation over standards of decency in movies, television, video games, and even music has long been part of the larger media-criticism landscape, particularly in the United States. And for just as long there have been organizations, formal and informal, ready to shield the public from a range of "objectionable" content, from a plucked and naked Tweety Bird in 1942 to use of the word "pregnant" on *I Love Lucy* in 1952, and from Elvis' gyrating pelvis on *The Ed Sullivan Show* to fresh-faced Mary Ann's bared navel on *Gilligan's Island*. These well-intentioned purveyors of virtue stand ready to inflict their own brand of decency on the public at large.

Violence has had its own special place on the hit lists of TV's would-be censors, second only to sexually provocative content. There were concerns as far back as the 1950s and early 1960s about the violence in television series such as *The Rifleman* and *The Untouchables*. Critics also took aim at movies being rerun on the tube—initially war films, Westerns, and gangster films, and later, martial arts films. Congress held its first hearings on television violence all the way back in 1952. A year later, the Subcommittee to Investigate Juvenile Delinquency was formed, and subsequent congressional hearings on the topic of television violence were staged throughout the 1950s and 1960s, continuing on through the turn of the century. These hearings often veered off into testimony on other media, including comic books, which were special targets in the McCarthy-era 1950s, thanks in no small part to Dr. Fredric Wertham's 1954 book *Seduction of the Innocent*. While Wertham is known these days primarily as a critic of comics, *Seduction* also included a section

entitled "Homicide at Home," which details the perils of television violence and its connection to juvenile delinquency.

The year 1964 brought an entirely new dimension to the public's concern about violent content, as the country began to question the mass media consumed by a society that had allowed
its president to be assassinated. The 60 million Americans who
owned televisions in the 1960s, up from 10 million in 1950,
found in the glowing boxes a portal through which a turbulent
decade invaded their lives. They turned on their sets nightly to
images of violent street demonstrations tied to the civil rights
movement, political assassinations, and the military carnage of
the Vietnam War, all beamed directly into their living rooms. This
rebellious era was the game-changer in our cultural desensitization to violence. The advent of color television only increased
the appeal of the bloodshed, grounding it in Technicolor reality
and fascinating the millions of average working-class Americans
whose lives by that time had settled into relatively stable schedules of shift work and domesticity.

Still, well-intentioned alarmists, such as Tipper Gore's infamous Parents Music Resource Center, continued to combat
violent content where they could, particularly through the introduction of both age- and content-based ratings designations.
The ratings are supposed to allow consumers to locate content
they consider suitable for themselves and their families. With the
passage of the Parental Choice in Television Programming Act of
1996, the government mandated V-chip technology be installed
in all new sets, allowing parents to block content based on their
ratings. But the designations also had other consequences. They
made it easier for viewers to locate the shows most likely to
bring them the level of violence they wanted to see. Particularly
for younger viewers, who tend to be more tech savvy than their
parents and able to work around artificial barriers such as the

V-chip, these ratings systems act as dangling carrots leading them right to the forbidden fruits, now helpfully labeled "TV-MA."

The allure of forbidden content is no less strong for today's younger consumers than it was for the 1950s teen sneaking down to a darkened living room at midnight to watch *The Vampira Show*. The only difference is that younger viewers no longer have to sneak around to gain access to it. Readily available streaming content on the internet transforms computers and iPhones into high-tech theaters of the Grand Guignol.

A case could certainly be made that the changing function of the television itself has blurred the lines between standalone entertainment medium and conduit. No longer is the screen's sole purpose to receive television shows; it now acts as a monitor through which video games are played, movies are rented and screened, and the internet is accessed, with everything that access entails. No rating system or censoring body can ever really cover the myriad shows, games, movies, YouTube videos, news sites, and blog posts that someone might view on the screen in the house still quaintly referred to as "the television." And since television as a concept has evolved, in practical use, beyond a distinct distribution channel with tightly controlled, family-friendly content, the consumer's idea of what is acceptable "on TV" has evolved, too.

So when the zombies of *The Walking Dead* tear an arm off a member of the ensemble cast, it's likely to barely register as remarkable when viewed on the same screen on which video game characters are graphically and repeatedly slain during interactive shootouts. Few will blink when Grimes' ill-fated horse is torn apart on that downtown city street after they've watched high-definition shots of war causalities in Afghanistan. And thus, for all its unrepentant bloodletting bravado, *The Walking Dead* is probably not nearly as much a button-pushing show as *NYPD Blue* once was. After all, even a gore-spattered Waldo won't stand out if all the people crowding around him are just as bloody.

It's important to keep in mind, too, that violence takes a backseat to sex and nudity on television on the "outrage and uproar" scale. Indeed, parents are more likely to cover little Timmy's eyes when Janet Jackson suffers a wardrobe malfunction during halftime at the Super Bowl than when half the cast of *The Walking Dead* reach into the disemboweled remains of a dead zombie and drape the entrails all over their bodies. To put it more bluntly: Number of FCC complaints over Jackson's "Nipplegate"—540,000. Number of FCC complaints over *The Walking Dead*'s violence to date—I challenge you to find one. I couldn't.

Flash back to 2003: the FCC has just levied a $27,500 fine against the ABC network and its affiliate stations for airing an episode of *NYPD Blue* in which actress Charlotte Ross' bare buttocks were shown before 10:00 p.m. Flash forward seven years: a federal appeals court strikes down that penalty. Seven years, one naked derrière. Conversely, that same noted police drama routinely depicted physical violence, including police brutality and realistic crime scenes with plenty of blood, with little to no brouhaha. You can thank the enduring repressed Puritan influence of our founding forefathers for that logic.

The Walking Dead's berth on the primetime schedule also has some bearing in this examination of its level of violence and the public's reaction to it. Despite the groundbreaking push of *NYPD Blue* and ABC's short-lived Chicago crime drama *Lady Blue* (1985–86) toward grittier depictions of violence, would Darabont and Co. get away with even one of those close-range gunshots to the head that seem commonplace on the show if *The Walking Dead* were on network TV? Imagine the thunderstruck reactions of the network censors in the Divisions of Standards and

Practices at the Peacock Network or the Disney-ABC Television Group if they were to watch as Officer Grimes wanders through a wasteland of deserted cars, confronts a snarling zombie child, and delivers a single gunshot to the little girl's head. Sure, let's bookend this between *Survivor* and *The Mentalist*.

Conversely, would *The Walking Dead*'s brutality even be a topic of discussion if it followed the violent vampires of HBO's *True Blood* on Sunday nights? Despite *The Walking Dead* seeming a perfect fit for the creative freedoms offered by pay-cable programming—in fact, at one time the show was attached to HBO as a Guillermo Del Toro project—it was the basic cable outlet AMC that acquired the project. AMC, like its FX, TNT, and Syfy brethren, is one of those broadcast middlemen, not expected to either hold to the fastidious decency restrictions of the three major networks or succumb to the "anything goes" mantra of the premium pay-cable outlets such as HBO or Showtime.

Basic cable, the weird no-man's-land between network TV and subscription entertainment, blurs that hard divide between the safety of policed network fare and the edginess of less restrictive pay-cable outlets. *The Walking Dead* takes full advantage of this distortion and switches the game up a bit. It swings the pendulum (or in its case, an axe) decidedly toward pay-TV standards with its unrestrained blood, guts, and gore on a network broadcast into the homes of almost everyone with basic cable. That cable identity helps temper the pushback *The Walking Dead* might otherwise receive. And with the show's ratings and critical success—capped off with a refreshingly unexpected Golden Globe Award nomination for "Best Drama" in its inaugural season—look for even the more mainstream networks to slip in edgier fare like *The Walking Dead* onto their ailing primetime schedules.

While the latitude afforded cable programming and the overall cultural desensitization to television violence fostered by the increased functionality of the television itself dilute some of the shock elicited by gore and mayhem flashing across an ever-enlarging screen, the strength of *The Walking Dead*'s narrative focus is the most important factor in determining the public's reaction to its content. The story at the show's core helps inform a perspective on the violence, violence that impacts the narrative but never really permeates or overshadows it.

During the fourth episode of season one, the survivors' camp suffers a brutal nighttime assault by a zombie mob. Although there was little restraint on the visceral intensity of the episode's well-choreographed nocturnal fight scene, it was the resulting causalities—particularly that of the winsome Amy on the eve of her birthday—that packed the real emotional punch. In addition to giving actress Laurie Holden, who plays older sister Andrea, some career-best work for her demo reel, it was a warning jolt for audiences. Amy and Andrea are seen fishing at the beginning of the episode, reminiscing about their father and savoring the bonds of their sisterhood; by show's end, less than twenty-four hours later in the story's timeline, one sister has succumbed to her zombie-inflicted injuries and the other is left to mourn her loss. Don't get too attached to anyone, the writers seem to be saying, because everyone's expendable at the end of the world.

Acts of violence are germane to the story itself—this *is* a zombie apocalypse, after all—and not splashy add-ons meant simply to shock and titillate. In this sense, any claims that might be leveled against the show for "excessive" violence are empty. The mayhem is quite necessary for the tale that's being told. Although the violence is prevalent, it falls far short of being sustained.

And while gorehounds may be attracted to the show's inevitable bounty of zombie violence each week, they shouldn't be surprised to find themselves invested in the fates of the characters.

Unlike the typical zombie opus—or, worse, the horror genre's much-maligned slasher film—in which the terms "cast of characters" and "body count" are interchangeable, *The Walking Dead* isn't a show about the dead rising to feed on the living; it's a show about the living's reaction to the dead rising to feed on them. Genuine drama ensues when characters must either adapt to the extreme circumstances forced upon them or perish. The look of shock and devastation on Rick Grimes' face when he shoots that little undead girl wearing the bunny slippers is an understated yet powerful reflection of the survivor's inner devastation—and it's the relatable characters digging through this mental wreckage that ultimately drive the show.

In this context, the violence of *The Walking Dead* would be secondary to character development and exposition. But is it really? Are all the exploding heads and flesh-eating merely bursts of extreme violence punctuating the ghostly stillness of a cadaverous landscape razed by the living embodiment of death? The violence *is* important because it frames the narrative in such unyieldingly bleak and punishing circumstances, which only makes the human interaction, action, and reaction to the unfolding events all the more pronounced, ultimately heightening the audience's response to and expectations of the show's characters.

The violence of *The Walking Dead*, while not its central focus, is essential to the show's success as storytelling. Without it, the emotional investment stemming from our empathetic response to the situations in which these characters find themselves would be missing. Extreme violence, in the case of *The Walking Dead*, actually enhances the tale being told rather than serving as window-dressing extravagance.

VINCE A. LIAGUNO is an award-winning writer, anthologist and editor, and an occasional poet. Vince won the Bram Stoker Award for *Unspeakable Horror: From the Shadows of the Closet* (Dark Scribe Press, 2008), which he co-edited with Chad Helder. His debut novel, 2006's *The Literary Six*, won an Independent Publisher Award (IPPY) for Horror and was named a finalist in *ForeWord Magazine*'s Book of the Year Awards in the Gay/Lesbian Fiction category. Vince most recently served as editor on *Butcher Knives & Body Counts* (Dark Scribe Press, 2011), a collection of essays on the slasher film. He is a member—and current secretary—of the Horror Writers Association and the National Book Critics Circle. Online at vinceliaguno.com.

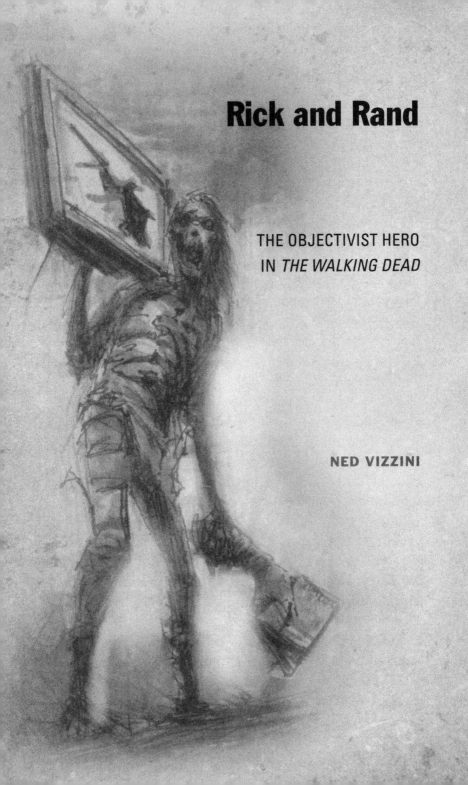

Rick and Rand

THE OBJECTIVIST HERO
IN *THE WALKING DEAD*

NED VIZZINI

The apocalypse is not going anywhere. After thwarting our attempts to bring it about in Y2K, it went dormant, built up buzz, and resurfaced as the Mayan transformation of 2012, which has taken over entire sections of chain bookstores. (If you are thinking ahead, you may want to check out *2013: Raising the Earth to the Next Vibration*.) When 2012 comes and goes, human beings are sure to fixate on another end, perhaps exhuming Nostradamus' stale supermarket predictions or falling back on the comfortingly un-outlandish but no less dramatic scenarios of climate change, terrorism, and plague. The apocalypse is compelling to us—sexy, even. As Chuck Palahniuk observes in *Lullaby*, "Every generation wants to be the last."

Why are humans so fascinated, across cultures and religions, with our end? Is it self-importance, as Palahniuk implies? Is it the communal manifestation of the individual death wishes that make us smoke, or drink, and purchase books such as *2013: Raising the Earth to the Next Vibration*? While these are factors, *The Walking Dead,* both the comic and TV series, illustrates that the biggest draw of the apocalypse is the way it absolves us of our responsibilities.

In the twenty-first century, we live lives burdened by crushing, metastasizing obligations: to our bodies, our clothes, our homes, our cars, our jobs, our kids, our internet presence. The apocalypse offers us a chance to erase all of these and scale life back to one responsibility—*staying alive*. We can be like the heroes in

Trainspotting, who forgo all earthly concerns to do heroin, but nobler, without the heroin. We want the world to end, in short, because we do not want to pay the cable bill.

Robert Kirkman's zombie epic began in 2003, between our era's two most compelling apocalyptic fantasies: 9/11 and the 2008 financial crisis. It is at its best when illustrating the unexpected positives of living in a world overrun with zombies. High-flying Glenn, who can duck in and out of Atlanta for supplies like Spider-Man, explains that before the zombie uprising, "I was . . . pizza delivery boy." Carol, nestled with a book in the arms of her lover Tyreese, muses, "I didn't realize how much I *missed* reading. It's funny how we don't really realize the things we're missing." Much later in the series, Rick Grimes, our hero, realizes he can use the apocalypse to surround himself with the right people and create lasting communal good.

Along with these unexpected positives, however, comes the brutal reality of day-to-day survival. Here *The Walking Dead* pulls no punches and earns its most bloodthirsty fans. Its violence is not unprecedented—read *Preacher*, a comic series that ran from 1995 to 2000, and bemoan the loss of the "Preacher Grievous Head-Wound Count" fan website—but its multitude of shifting personalities and lack of sacred cows ensures that *anyone* is liable to get killed or kill at any time.

That includes children: Rick teaches his son, Carl, to shoot a gun as soon as he can; Carl goes to work offing zombies and then Shane, Rick's best friend. Shortly after, Carl is shot by Otis; he later murders Ben, a sociopathic child. He begins as a grade-schooler but the apocalypse gives him the resume of a Nigerian child-warrior. He develops the countenance of one, too, after getting part of his head blown off in issue eighty-three.

In response to this violence and brutality, many of *The Walking Dead*'s survivors try to cling to their old ways—until circumstances force them to give them up. Hershel insists that God is looking out for him until he begs Him for death. Lori defends her right to raise Carl free of violence as if the zombies had never appeared ("I guess the end of the world means I've no longer got a *say* in parenting my own *son*," she protests to Rick), but she is living a fantasy. "We have these *small talk* questions," she eventually admits. "Do you have kids? Where do your parents live? [. . .] They just don't work anymore." *The Walking Dead*'s world is a changed one, and the imperatives of surviving in an apocalypse require a fresh look at reality, including responsibility.

Who am I responsible for after the end of the world? This question falls squarely on the shoulders of Rick. Does he need to worry only about himself? His family? Does society as a whole have a place in his concerns?

Comics themselves have been grappling with this issue since their inception. Early heroes such as Captain America were responsible for their countries. *Spider-Man* brought us perhaps the most well-known comic book bromide—"with great power comes great responsibility"—and is built on the idea that a normal person, granted extraordinary skills, cannot be responsible solely for himself. (I use "himself" in place of "him- or herself" for the duration of this essay, in a nod to Ayn Rand, who always sticks to the male pronoun.)

The Walking Dead gives readers a chance to see the *true* nature of responsibility in a world gone mad, including the dangers of accepting too much of it. The way it addresses heroism and responsibility allows us to analyze it through the lens of not just comics but Objectivism, which grew up alongside comics in the twentieth century.

When we talk about Objectivism, we have to talk about Ayn Rand, and this makes a lot of people uncomfortable. Rand has become a neoconservative icon, beloved by corporate titans who use her ideas as intellectual justification for cutthroat capitalism, but examination of her writing shows that her politics is secondary to her undeniably popular way of looking at the world. She called this view "Objectivism"; she wanted to call it "existentialism" but Sartre got there first.

Thinking of Objectivism as existentialism is helpful. Rand's philosophy relies, first and foremost, on existence, on the primacy of the real world. Her novel *Atlas Shrugged*, which Rand scholar Leonard Peikoff calls "her magnum opus [devoted] to the fundamentals of philosophy" (at 1,168 pages, it had better be), exhorts that "A is A," which may seem obvious but in philosophical thought is by no means a given. Many thinkers hold that reality is a construct of the human mind, that perception of an event makes it real, and that any A can be B if the person observing it hails from a different culture or has a different idea of what A and B mean. Rand rejects all of this. "Existence exists," says her über-hero John Galt. "You cannot have your cake and eat it too."

To survive in the real world, then, where things exist that are not manifestations of human consciousness, men must use *reason*. "Since nature does not provide man with an automatic form of survival [. . .] he has to support his life by his own effort," Rand explains in *The Virtue of Selfishness*. Reason—meaning deductive logic of the Aristotelian school—is the only tool that humans can use to extract a livelihood from the world around them, which is indifferent to them and unswayed by their emotions, prayers, or "whims," a word Rand particularly detested.

"In order to sustain its life, every living species has to follow a certain course of action required by its nature," she writes in *Capitalism: The Unknown Ideal*. "The action required to sustain human life is primarily intellectual: everything man needs has to be discovered by his mind and produced by his effort. Production is the application of reason to the problem of survival."

We may not think of Rick Grimes as an intellectual, but his relentless application of reason to the world around him has ensured his survival thus far. If he had ever believed that he could parley with the zombies, that they were not monsters, that A was not A, that by wishing and hoping he could achieve a better life, he would be long gone. Hershel, through religion, tries to whitewash the new reality and ends up dead. Rick's adherence to reason even when it requires unthinkable action keeps him going.

Objectivism supports the freedom of men to pursue their own interests, to be selfish. Thus it dovetails laissez-faire capitalism and stands against all forms of collectivism—especially communism, whose supporters Rand fled at age twelve. In U.S. politics, Rand supported Republicans, but there is a perception that her love of free markets condones a dog-eat-dog, kill-or-be-killed attitude, and this is furthest from the truth.

She detested violence. She saw it as the barbaric result of men failing to listen to reason. "A civilized society is one in which physical force is banned from human relationships—in which the government, acting as a policeman, may use force *only* in retaliation and *only* against those who initiate its use," she writes in *Capitalism*. Her distinction between initiatory and retaliatory force is echoed by Rick when he devises his "you kill, you die" rule after he discovers Thomas' murder of Hershel's girls. Violence is only acceptable in response to other violence—which proves a difficult doctrine to enforce.

The philosophy of Objectivism is about the same age as the comic book, and the two have come together in unexpected ways over the past fifty years. One of the best-known Rand adherents is Steve Ditko, *Spider-Man*'s co-creator and original illustrator, who left Marvel in 1966 to pursue work of a more philosophical bent. He created superheroes such as Mr. A, an undisguised Objectivist polemicist, and concocted 1973's truly insane (and beautiful) *The Avenging World*, a free-form exploration of Objectivist ideas with a "Skeptical Intellectual" character who says, "Take it from ONE WHO KNOWS, NOBODY can KNOW ANYTHING FOR CERTAIN!" Ditko, "an artist whose principles have ossified into bitter perversity," according to *The New York Times*, remains distanced from *Spider-Man* and has been absent from public appearances for decades.

Perhaps it is for the best. "With great power comes great responsibility" is not a phrase an Objectivist would agree with. For Rand and Ditko, great power brings the same thing that little power brings: the right of men to pursue their own interests through rational thought.

One comic book writer who did take note of Ditko's Objectivist creations was Alan Moore, who patterned Rorschach of *Watchmen* after Ditko's Randian hero The Question. In a mask that echoes The Question's, Rorschach opines that there are good and evil in the world, that the evil is *unquestionably* evil, that it deserves to be punished, and that its punishment is to be meted out by him according to the reason of right and wrong, not some wishy-washy government.

This intellectual definitiveness imbues Rick Grimes as well. Although he, unlike Rorschach, has a family, he shares the masked hero's belief in the primacy of existence, the right of him and his fellow survivors to pursue their own interests, and the punishable sin of initiating violence. In these ways, he is an Objectivist hero attempting to make sense of his new responsibilities in a changed world. But his emotional instability and violent streak threaten to undo him.

Rick may not appear to be an Objectivist hero at first. He identifies most strongly and frequently as a cop. A cursory knowledge of objectivism might lead a reader to think this makes him a tool of the state; however, Rand argues otherwise. Law enforcement is one of the only state responsibilities she defends, in "Moral Inflation," along with the courts and the military. It is acceptable from an Objectivist perspective—honorable even—for Rick to uphold the law, which by all accounts he does competently, if not thrillingly, before getting shot on the first page of *The Walking Dead.*

When he wakes up on the next page, Rick is plunged into the fantasy of the apocalypse and quickly finds himself in the nightmare. Note how adaptable he is: he abandons what Rand would cite as non-Objectivist cop roles, the old duties no longer applicable to upholding the basic functions of "protect and serve." When Duane confesses that he has been squatting in a neighbor's house, Rick does not arrest him; instead he offers him a police car. "I can't think of a better way to *'protect and serve'* under the circumstances," he says. Later, with Glenn, he steals guns, carrying out a crime he would have punished in a past life. He holds true to the spirit of the law but tailors it to the world around him, at least until personal tragedy makes him reevaluate his responsibility to anyone but his family. Family is the only thing more important to Rick than his job. His reunion with Carl and Lori at camp—*The Walking Dead*'s first unexpected, indelible moment—lays the foundation for the series' drama. Rick now has his wife and kid to think about. He takes on this additional responsibility thankfully, blessedly. Unlike Rorschach, he has someone to protect.

Rick settles in well at camp. He fulfills the role of order provider and family protector through the savage, pretechnological imperative of hunting and learns to live without walls and a roof. ("Civilization is the progress toward a society of privacy," Rand writes in *The Fountainhead.* "The savage's whole existence is public.") His familiarity with guns and violence prepares him for the new normal in a way that the other survivors lack, though many quickly learn—such as law clerk-cum-sharpshooter Andrea. There are moments of real peace for him, such as when he awakens in his tent, sees Lori and Carl, and rubs Lori's shoulder lovingly, as if to make sure she is real.

It is when Rick extends his responsibility beyond himself and his family—when he becomes a caretaker for the *group*—that trouble begins.

Objectivism has a specific term for responsibility toward others. Some call it "kindness," or "giving back," or "being a good person," but Objectivism calls it "altruism"—and despises it. Altruism stands in opposition to the rational self-interest that Rand believed was man's best motivator. She saw it only as a tool used by parasites to take advantage of the productive capacity of others. "No creator was prompted by a desire to serve his brothers," she writes in *The Fountainhead*. "His truth was his only motive."

Does Rick share this view? Not at first. His early impulse in *The Walking Dead* is to care for others, by teaching them to shoot, for example. This may seem like a no-brainer—people have to defend themselves—but a convincing argument could be made for keeping guns *out* of the hands of scared, irrational survivors following a zombie apocalypse. More than once people fire guns foolishly and draw the walkers; Rick's own son is shot by a stray bullet twice (so far). When the armed-and-ready survivors encounter Tyreese, their first outsider, Rick continues his altruistic streak by offering shelter and support for nothing in return. His wife chastises him for being too soft. He provides Hershel with firearms and invites him to come stay at the prison; once there, when he discovers four living inmates, he absolves them of their past wrongs and accepts them into the group. This bit of kindness incenses Lori. Rick argues, "They *seem* like nice enough people." "No, Rick," she responds, "they *seem* like *hardened criminals.*"

Perhaps Rick is motivated by enlightened self-interest. Objectivism does not mean having to do everything solo. Individuals can enter into agreements for mutual benefit—but it is up to each individual to be diligent in deciding whom to partner with. Rick later seems to conclude that a safe society is possible if he picks the right people, and as a reward for taking on added responsibility, he has a chance to pick those people. He is made the leader of the group. Dale explains, "We need someone to look up to . . . to make us feel *safe*, especially the women [. . .] We think that someone is *you*." Rick does not protest.

But now he is responsible for a dozen survivors with wildly disparate backgrounds, skills, and secrets. When Hershel's daughters are killed, Rick admits to his wife, "It's all *my fault*, Lori. Those girls are *dead* because of *me*." He is no longer a man trying to survive by his own reason. He is a leader responsible for others who must make life-and-death decisions—ethical decisions.

In her talk "The Objectivist Ethics," Ayn Rand defines ethics and morality as synonyms—"a code of values to guide man's choices and actions." It is on this (shifting) "code of values" that Rick attempts to rely as he leads the survivors. His struggle to be fair and effective is contrasted with the amorality—the null ethics—of the zombie majority, the cannibal hunters, and Father Gabriel Stokes, who should be responsible but fails his followers, an example that would satisfy the dismissive Objectivist view of religion. The walkers, roamers, and biters have no need for ethics. "Try to imagine an immortal, indestructible robot, an entity which moves and acts, but which cannot be affected by anything," Rand says. "Such an entity would not be able to have any values; it would have nothing to gain or to lose." Did someone slip her a few *Walking Dead* trades?

Rick modifies his ethics to fit his new reality, continuing the adaptability he shows early in the series. "I may be a cop," he says, "but I don't let rules *blind* me to what's right and wrong." At first, this works for him, but by trusting his instincts, he begins to rely on his feelings rather than look at the world around him and recognize objective truth.

While upholding the law as a police officer, Rick supports an accepted external morality. When he makes up new rules, he submits his morality to his *internal*, subjective motivations—a deadly mistake for an Objectivist hero. After all, who is he to judge? Rand writes, in *The Virtue of Selfishness*, "To pronounce moral judgment is an enormous responsibility. To be a judge, one must possess an unimpeachable character." Does Rick have the character necessary to take on such responsibility? Absolutely not. He may start out with it, but it soon unravels. His emotions—the whims that Rand so distrusts—overtake his rational processes.

Rick's threshold act is the killing of Thomas, the prisoner who beheads Hershel's girls. Rick ends his life not with a gun, cleanly, but with a brutal beating. In doing so, he moves from the clean logic of protecting his own to the emotional murk of revenge. Instead of imprisoning or exiling Thomas, he initiates passionate force—and then claims that he did so out of *a sense of responsibility to his community*. "I'm the *only* one here in a position of *authority*. *I'm* making the choice that's *best* for *all* of us," he tells Lori. Really, Rick is using his crime of passion to enshrine his power: "*I'm in charge.*"

Thus Rick inches from rational, self-reliant survivor to autocrat. His murder of Thomas shades him toward an Attila figure, outlined by Rand in her essay "Attila and the Witch Doctor," as a "man of force" who gains power "whenever men abandon reason." *The Walking Dead* is full of Attilas, showing us a society in which force rules all—but until Rick resorts to emotion-based thuggery, he is not one of them. Afterward, as judge, jury, and executioner, his moral position is more difficult to defend.

Not that Rick doesn't try. He attempts to come up with a new rule after killing Thomas: "*You kill. You die.*" He uses this justification to explain himself to Tyreese, who is also a murderer but who does not try to justify his actions as being because of others. Rick's rule does not last long, however—he breaks it dispassionately when he kills Dexter, a troublesome prisoner, with a gun in a moment of opportunity. Tyreese sees this second murder and calls Rick out on it: "Kinda throws the whole '*You kill, you die*' thing out the window, huh?" The topic of Rick's use of power arises again between the two men after Carol's suicide attempt. This time it results in a knock-down, drag-out fight, the prevention of which is one of Rand's sole justifications for a state. Logically neutered, Rick can only respond with force. The truth is that Dexter's murder and similar actions have cannibalized his morality.

Rick falls back on the power granted him by the group: "You people *put* me in charge. I've been asked to shoulder the responsibilities of everyone here—and I've taken it upon myself to keep everyone *safe*." And then, "Everything I did—*everything*—I did for the good of this group [. . .] That's what makes me right." This statement violates all the principles of the Objectivist hero. Instead of a rational man relying on reason, Rick is now a straw man relying on the mob, an Attila on the level of his soon-to-be nemesis, the Governor.

The Governor is one of *The Walking Dead*'s most enduring figures, ranked number eighty-six on IGN's 2009 "Top 100 Comic Book Villains of All Time." He is a perverted vision of

Rand's Attila, who rules by force and can bring only savagery, but he is also quite similar to Rick.

The Governor is a leader. He keeps his people safe. He runs a community as Rick does—a much larger one, in fact. Most important, *he uses his community responsibility to justify his actions.* Torturing? Killing? It's not that the Governor likes these things; he is merely preserving the safety of his people. Stalin used the same excuses.

Rick's battle with the Governor bookends *The Walking Dead*'s first indelible moment with its most tragic frame, in which Lori and baby Judith are shot. Following his wife's death, Rick *is* able to lead his people to defeat the Governor (with the help of some zombies), but then the horror really starts.

After being pursued by the cannibalistic hunters following his flight from the prison, Rick tortures and kills those who threaten his group. In a silent montage of grisly vengeance, he *becomes* the Governor before our eyes, and Kirkman turns Stan Lee's old chestnut on its head. Yes, with great power comes responsibility—but with the responsibility of leadership comes great power. And this power can corrupt.

All is not lost for Rick as an Objectivist hero. Following his fight with Tyreese, he begins to give up his role as judge, jury, and executioner by accepting Dale's announcement of the committee that has been formed to govern the survivors. He also remains proactive and rationally engaged throughout his hardships. When he learns that Martinez, one of the Governor's men, has gone back to the Governor in Woodbury to reveal the location of the prison, he does not delegate the task of capturing him to an underling. He tracks Martinez down himself—and upon finding him illustrates a newfound indifference toward altruism.

Martinez whines: "You *selfish* piece of *shit*. You've got the room—the supplies for *everyone in Woodbury*—the whole *damn* town! [. . .] My people *deserve* to be *safe*, too." Rick dismisses his need-based argument. He kills Martinez and confesses to Lori, "I used to be a trained police officer [. . .] Now I feel more like a lawless *savage*—an *animal*." The lawmaker can no longer see the law—can no longer see A for A.

Rick falls short of Ayn Rand's high standards—but then again, everyone does. Rand writes, in *The Romantic Manifesto*, "The motive and purpose of my writing is *the projection of an ideal man*," and Rick is far from ideal. Unlike Howard Roark, or Hank Rearden, or John Galt, Rick Grimes is not a tireless adherent to the force of reason; he is an ordinary man caught up in extraordinary times struggling with the seductive evil and crushing pressure of new responsibility. He is not a spotless hero, as his surname implies. He cannot shake the grime of the world.

While Rand notes that "popular fiction does not raise or answer abstract questions," she would be hard pressed to sideline *The Walking Dead* as belonging to "the literary cult of depravity" (her term for horror fiction). The concerns of *The Walking Dead* resonate with readers in part because they reflect our own concerns about the fate of America—concerns Rand shared.

Rand warned that America would succumb to the walking dead, but it was intellectual zombie-ism she feared. In *Philosophy: Who Needs It*, published in 1982, she says:

> Today, the concerted effort of our cultural "Establishment" is directed at the obliteration of man's rational faculty. Hysterical voices are proclaiming the impotence of reason [. . .] glorifying the stupor of drugged hippies, delivering apologies for the use of brute force, urging mankind's return to a life of rolling in primeval muck, with grunts and groans as a means of communication [. . .] and a club as a means of argumentation.

Rick's Objectivist identity is still in flux. He backslides and picks up the club throughout *The Walking Dead* but never as viciously as in its later issues, such as when he cuts off Jessie's hand to save Carl in the pivotal "No Way Out" story arc. Following that exchange, he has a revelation in which he envisions a society living *with* the walkers instead of finding somewhere devoid of them, a new community focused on rebuilding civilization instead of merely surviving. He is willing to enter into contracts for mutual benefit with his fellow survivors and take their suggestions rather than lording over them as an Attila, but his long list of moral failings, from murdering Thomas to cutting off Jessie's hand, leaves him difficult to trust. Rand writes in *For the New Intellectual* that the "new intellectual" will be the man "who is guided by his *intellect*—not a zombie guided by feelings, instincts, urges, wishes, whims or revelations." Would she see Rick as a hero or a zombie? The fact that he teeters between the two is what makes him a figure for our own apocalyptic age.

NED VIZZINI is the author of three acclaimed young adult books: *It's Kind of a Funny Story* (also a major motion picture), *Be More Chill*, and *Teen Angst? Naaah* . . . Ned has spoken at over 200 schools, universities, libraries, and organizations around the world about writing and mental health. He has written for *The New York Times*, *Writer's Digest*, and *L Magazine*. His work has been translated into seven languages. His next novel, *The Other Normals*, will be published in fall 2012. Online at nedvizzini.com.

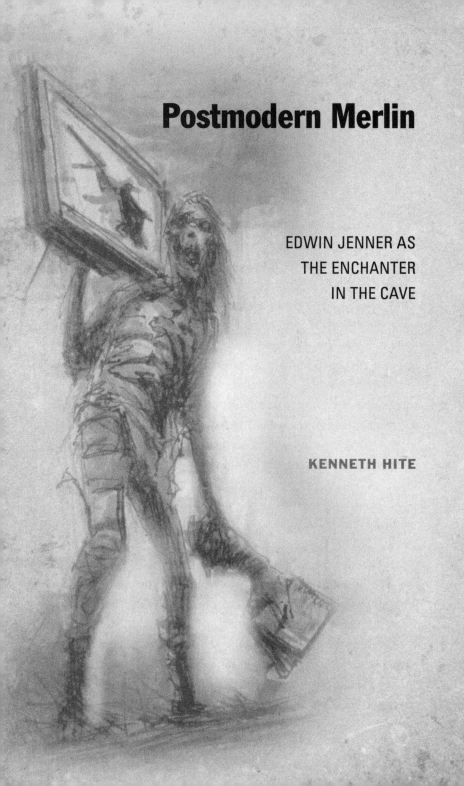

Postmodern Merlin

EDWIN JENNER AS
THE ENCHANTER
IN THE CAVE

KENNETH HITE

A scientist in an underground bunker. A wizard in a crypt. Both are instantly recognizable figures from film and fiction: we feel as if we already know their story when they appear. We have seen them before, again and again in different contexts and costumes. Change the costumes: put the white lab coat on the wizard or the star-embroidered robe on the scientist. Back behind the figure in the dim light, give the scrying stone a keyboard and a Macintosh veneer; change the gleaming retorts and beakers to bubbling cauldrons and alembics. Grow the obsessive tech nerd's stubble out into the wizard's beard; the sorcerer's diamantine gaze eventually shimmers into the scientist's spectacles. They are more than kin; they are the same. We have uncovered an archetype: the Enchanter in the Cave.

ARCHETYPE AND APOCALYPSE

Myths comprise multiple sets of stories: variations on a theme or even of a single hero tale. The myth of King Arthur encompasses scores of different adventures and varying versions of the same quests, betrayals, and battles. Each mythic story, meanwhile, from the Old Testament to the *Star Wars* saga, contains a string of events, characters, or items that folklorists call motifs, or mythemes—Jonah and the whale or Luke and the Death Star. Some of these mythemes recur in later myths, in myths from other traditions, or in the enormous mass of film and fiction influenced by mythology: Orestes, Frankenstein's monster, and Jason Bourne all seek both vengeance, by killing or trying to kill their creators, and self-knowledge.

According to Carl Jung, a particularly strong, common, or interesting mytheme—such as the Unwilling Hero or the Huntress—is often called an archetype, a Platonic term meaning the "ideal type" of an object. This can lead to some confusion, since archetypes vary as much as myths do. Although they hold a core thread through countless variations, there are few (or even no) unambiguously universal mythemes, implying instead that mythemes are culturally constructed at some level—perhaps centuries ago or within the creative subconscious of any given artist. The individual mythemes and their specific variants might come from religious belief or broad cultural tradition, or from a sociological (or neurological) predilection toward telling stories a certain way. Mythemes, in short, may simply be exciting habits rather than mystical truths. Their nature and origin matter less than their existence and what form they may take in any given myth.

As Ray Stantz reminds us in *Ghostbusters*, "Every ancient religion has its own myth about the end of the world"—from Revelation to Ragnarök to the quenching of the Fifth Sun. Our modern, secular culture is no exception to Stantz' rule. Our end-times myths vary with events: the nuclear holocaust has dampened into the warm smother of global warming. But neither of those is our true mythic end of the world. No, our end time is zombie time. The way we describe it is mythical, even religious: the "zombie apocalypse." The word "apocalypse" means "opening up," or "revelation," and as works such as *The Walking Dead* demonstrate, the zombie apocalypse reveals to us our true nature: Do we die or fight? Are we lone wolves, or do we shepherd survivors as best we can? The *Walking Dead*

TV series deliberately echoes apocalyptic imagery. The scene in episode one ("Days Gone Bye") in which Rick emerges from the hospital surrounded by bagged bodies references not only, for example, Scarlett O'Hara at the siege of Atlanta witnessing the apocalyptic death of the old world of the South in *Gone with the Wind* but the Tarot image of the Last Judgment and Ezekiel standing over the valley of dry bones in the Old Testament. That episode also shows the aftermath of a local Ragnarök, a war at the end of the world: the overrun military units outside the hospital, echoed on a larger scale by the battle wreckage outside the CDC building in episode five ("Wildfire").

The zombie apocalypse, like those of the Bible or the Prose Edda, strips away all other questions; earthly status and quarrels become meaningless, and the only truths are those we bring out of the wreckage into the new revelation. In *The Walking Dead*, those truths are family, humanity, and a resolution to reject not just the dead past of commercials and taxes but the false certainties of our time: fatalism, cynicism, and materialism. The back covers of the *Walking Dead* trade paperback collections lay it out: "The world we knew is gone. The world of commerce and frivolous necessity has been replaced by a world of survival and responsibility."

In the first volume of the *Walking Dead* comics, Shane represents the past, convinced that the answer is to hunker down and wait for the government, the army, and the old world to reassert themselves. Rick represents the new world, the world of revelation, convinced that the old answers are dead; in the new world, seven-year-olds should carry guns and the army isn't coming back. The new world of the zombie apocalypse is not the New Jerusalem or Vanaheim of the Christian or Norse apocalypses. Not yet. The ruins of the old world are all around. Most importantly, the corpses of the old world refuse to lie down and admit that their world is gone. They compete blindly for flesh, glutting the cities and walking aimlessly in search of pure matter. Rick and the survivors—our modern mythic heroes—carry the seeds of the new world inside them, the all-important rejection of the dead past and the resolve to stay alive. To quote the back cover of the *Walking Dead* collections again: "In a world ruled by the dead, we are forced to finally start living."

One purpose of myth is not so much to provide answers in a didactic sense but to make sure we can hear the questions clearly. When the dead rise, whose side are you on? What does it take to kill you? To make you give up? Myths assure us that the impossible will happen, that the supernatural (or in our secular myth, merely the unnatural) world touches our lives, and therefore that these questions are relevant, even vital. Myth is not a separate phenomenon; it shares borders and features with folktale, fiction, ritual, history, and theology. It derives elements and practices from all of them and shares its own purposes in return. The myth of the zombie apocalypse as presented in *The Walking Dead* draws up elements and practices from the older wells of legend, including legendary archetypes.

FORMS OF THE ENCHANTER

Keeping in mind the plastic, even protean, nature of mythemes, we might ask: what does the Enchanter in the Cave look like? At his core, the Enchanter is someone with special knowledge—an artificer like Hephaestus of Greek mythology, a biblical prophet like Elijah, a supernatural being like the giant Mímir of Norse mythology, or a magician like Prospero in *The Tempest*. I use "his" because both Merlin and Edwin Jenner are male, but the Enchanter is female in many versions of the myth—for example, the nymph Calypso in *The Odyssey*, the prophetic Sibyl in

Roman legendary history, Venus in the Tannhäuser ballads, or the sorceress Melissa in *Orlando Furioso*.

These roles vary and blend in individual Enchanters. Hephaestus, for example, is the god of smiths and the divine artificer, building machines and weapons for gods and heroes, but he also serves as clever adviser to Zeus and as a plotter on his own account, discovering, for example, the facts about his parentage by building a chair that compels the truth from its user. The giant Mímir mostly acts as a dispenser of prophetic wisdom in the Norse Eddas, but in his incarnation as Mime in Wagner's *Ring* cycle, he builds the magical Tarnhelm, a helmet that allows the wearer to be invisible. Bucur, a Romanian wizard lurking in the caverns of Bucegi, creates an enchanted flute, and Vergil, the wizard who dwells under Vesuvius in medieval legend, is an artificer and a prophet as well.

What does the Enchanter do? What is his (or her) purpose in the myth? That, too, varies from tale to tale, but most commonly, the Enchanter provides a prophecy or other guidance to the hero. Sometimes, that unnatural aid takes the form of a spell, or even a magical tool or weapon; other times, it leads the hero into disaster even though the prophecy is correct. Legends and folklore abound with cave-dwelling, uncanny beings, named and unnamed. Such generic versions of the Enchanter—the dwarves of Teutonic folklore, the korrigans of Brittany, or the mouros of Galicia in Spain—combine all the Enchanter's aspects: artificer, knower of secrets, predatory captor.

The most powerful and influential avatar of the Enchanter in the Cave is Merlin. Even more than Shakespeare's Prospero, Merlin serves as the exemplar from which all later incarnations of the Enchanter—including Edwin Jenner—draw sustenance and shape. Although the central legend of Merlin the prophet, originally named Myrddin, comes out of Welsh myth and folktale, Merlin the magician is, in many ways, a deliberate literary construction, just like Prospero or Edwin Jenner. Over less than a century, between 1150 and 1230, three authors—Geoffrey of Monmouth, Robert de Boron, and the anonymous author of the *Prose Merlin*—assembled the story of Merlin's demonic birth, his advice and prophecies at the court of Arthur, and his imprisonment and death in a cave at the hands of his pupil and paramour Viviane.

The mythic Enchanter's parallels with Edwin Jenner in the *Walking Dead* television series suggest that Jenner is the Enchanter in our zombie apocalypse story. Jenner is a master of the arcane art of epidemiology—perhaps the secret to life or death in the aftermath of a zombie pestilence. He studies the infected walkers' flesh and reads their minds, at least as far as the MRI recordings will take him. In short, he is a scientific necromancer—literally, one who seeks knowledge from the dead. He is a prophet in that he prophesies that Rick will someday be less grateful for the chance to leave the CDC building. If Carl starts resembling his comics counterpart, Jenner's joke that Carl is the "least harmless" of the survivors may also turn prophetic.

The Enchanter dwells in a cave, or cavelike space, hidden from the sun and usually far from civilization. Hephaestus' volcano is at the edge of the Greek world in Sicily; the hollow mountain that entraps Tannhäuser, the Venusberg, lies in the middle of the wilderness. The cave may be surrounded by dangers; it almost always contains water and death. Mímir lives in a cave over a magic well. The wizard Shazam from the *Captain Marvel* comics dwells in an abandoned subway station, surrounded by the chained sins of mankind. The Graeae, or gray sisters, dwell in a black cavern among the dead and give Perseus prophetic aid. Bucur's cavern holds the petrified forms of women he has kidnapped, turned to stone by the magical river in his cave. The

Cave of Montesinos in Spanish legend holds the spirits of women turned to water by a wizard.

As we explore in the next section, Merlin's cave appears at both ends of his Arthurian career. Jenner's cave is the CDC bunker deep under Atlanta, in the middle of the wilderness that is the walker-plagued city. Like Merlin's prison in the *Suite du Merlin*, Jenner's cave is also a tomb, where scores of researchers committed suicide. And it is indeed a prison, with gates that open only to admit Rick's party of survivors.

Often, the male Enchanter has an uncanny female companion. Sometimes she is a servant, as with the mechanical maidens who serve the god Hephaestus beneath Mount Etna. Sometimes she is a captive, as with the shape-shifting Ialomita, captured by Bucur. Occasionally, she is even a captor, as is Viviane. Prospero has both a daughter (Miranda) and a supernatural companion (Ariel); although the play calls Ariel "he" twice, the character is often staged as female. In tales such as those of Viviane or Ialomita, there is a romantic, or at least lustful, element between the Enchanter and the female figure in the cave; female Enchanters such as Venus and Calypso likewise romantically entangle the male heroes of their myths, keeping them in the cave by the power of love as much as by their magic.

Viviane—who in various versions of the story is called Nimue, Niniane, or Nivienne—is one of the Ladies of the Lake; in some versions, she is also related to Merlin by blood. In all versions, Merlin falls in love with her. Jenner's companion in his cave is his own love, his dead wife. She remains with him in flesh until the disaster at the end of "Wildfire," and in MRI imagery (what Prospero would no doubt call an "airy spirit") after that. In addition, the relationship between Jenner and Vai, the female-voiced computer that runs the CDC building, is pure Prospero and Ariel, or Hephaestus and mechanical maiden.

The Enchanter sometimes has a special relationship with death: Calypso can make men immortal, the Greek goddess Hecate speaks to the dead, Mímir survives his own beheading, and the Libyan Sibyl continues to prophesy after her burial. In Cervantes' ironic version of the legend of the Cave of Montesinos, the Enchanter is both the elderly tour guide Montesinos and the dead hero Durandarte, who gives Don Quixote prophetic (and useless) advice from within his own tomb. The Enchanter's cave may be an explicit or implicit afterlife, like Venus' cavern in German legend, or merely a doorway to it, like Hecate's cave. This association with death often means the Enchanter is a predator or kidnapper, such as in the case of the warlock Bucur, Somerset's Witch of Wookey Hole (who curses lovers), or the cannibalistic hag Black Annis of Leicestershire. Even when the Enchanter means the hero no ill, the deadly cave may still hold known or unknown dangers.

Merlin lives backward from death to birth and has foreseen both his own death and that of Arthur. Jenner's connection with death is less ambiguous. Death surrounds him on all levels: emotionally, intellectually, and of course, physically. He studies death, dissecting the dead while besieged by zombies. He, too, has foreseen his own death and perhaps the death of other survivors—by high-impulse thermobaric fuel-air explosive (HIT) when the building's fuel gives out.

LE MORTE D'JENNER

Sir Thomas Malory completed Merlin's creation. Malory's *Le Morte d'Arthur*, despite its French name, is the consummate English-language version of the Arthurian cycle, reconciling dozens of earlier sources into one sprawling narrative. Completed in 1469–1470, as movable type was just spreading into England, it imprinted Malory's Merlin forever in the Western imagination. Two incidents in the career of Malory's Merlin especially reflect and illuminate the Enchanter in the Cave archetype: Merlin's role in the birth of Arthur and Merlin's imprisonment at the hands of Nimue. Both stories resonate throughout the brief, unhappy career of Edwin Jenner.

In Malory's tale, King Uther Pendragon of Britain covets the wife of Duke Gorlois of Cornwall, the beautiful Ygraine. Under a pretext, he declares war on Gorlois, who withdraws his wife to the castle of Tintagel in Cornwall. Uther seeks out Merlin, who promises to change Uther's shape to that of Gorlois, allowing him to lie with Ygraine. Further, Merlin prophesies that this liaison will produce a child, whom Merlin requests Uther hand over as the price for his aid. Uther agrees, and Merlin casts his spell. While Uther's men attack Gorlois, Uther enters Tintagel and sleeps with Ygraine, who believes him to be her husband. Gorlois dies three hours before they conceive Arthur, and the widowed Ygraine later marries the victorious Uther. Uther keeps his word and hands their child over to Merlin, who takes him away to raise.

This story originally comes from Geoffrey of Monmouth; Cornish legend (and the contemporary tourism board) identifies as Merlin's Cave a sea cave below Tintagel Castle. Note the combination of love and death in the Enchanter's activities; Merlin assists at both Ygraine's ravishing and, by his magical advice to Uther, at the death of her husband. This is the Enchanter as predator as well as adviser and wizard; reinforcing this image, Merlin also takes the infant for his own purposes.

Jenner's story parallels Merlin's on a symbolic level. The unwitting adultery of Ygraine echoes the unwitting adultery of Lori. While Jenner doesn't actively facilitate a rendezvous between Shane and Lori, Shane does attempt to rape her in Jenner's rec room. Lori and Shane's original liaison occurred while Lori believed her husband to be dead when he had actually survived—a subtle reversal of the Merlin tale, in which Ygraine believes her husband to be alive although he is actually dead.

Many years later, after Arthur has grown and assumed his throne, and after many quests and prophecies, Merlin meets a maiden, Nimue, at Arthur's court at Camelot and conceives a great passion for her. Nimue leads Merlin on, promising to become his lover after he teaches her his magical arts. Merlin then tells Arthur that he has foreseen Nimue arranging his own death. Arthur asks him to use his magic to survive instead, but Merlin refuses to change his fate or avert his own doom. So Nimue leaves Camelot with Merlin in tow, constantly putting off his lovesick appeals. Fearing his magic, she makes him swear never to harm her or take her by force. Eventually, they reach a wild place in Cornwall "in a rock whereas was a great wonder, and wrought by enchantment, that went under a great stone." Nimue urges Merlin to go under the stone, where she traps him in the cavern using the arts he taught her: "she wrought so there for him that he came never out for all the craft he could do."

The oldest known version of this story appears in the *Prose Merlin*. In this version, Viviane imprisons Merlin but comes back to check on him each day; her action seems almost defensive or weirdly affectionate. In the later *Suite du Merlin*, Nivienne traps Merlin not in a cavern but in a tomb that contained a pair of legendary lovers. In both versions, Merlin survives long enough to speak to passing knights and heroes but never acts to free himself. Here, the Enchanter, his cave, and the uncanny lover are apparent. In Malory's version especially, the Enchanter is trapped as much by his own prophetic abilities as he is by Nimue: he has seen his own inevitable fate, and to avoid it would be to negate his powers.

Here, Jenner's parallel with Merlin is more direct. He, too, is trapped in a cave and foresees his own inevitable death. He, too, went to the cave with his lover to practice the mysterious arts—epidemiology, not magic, but how different are they in a world full of walking dead? Like Merlin, Jenner is held in his cave not by force but by his oath to his lover, in this case his dead wife. Like Merlin, he has made peace with the inevitable death he has seen in his future. Jenner can speak to passing heroes but never acts to free himself. The show reverses Malory by having Jenner's wife be his superior in the relevant arcane art, but the teacher-pupil relationship remains to illustrate the parallels.

Jenner is not a mere Merlin clone. He echoes other aspects of the Enchanter in the Cave, as well. His prophetic warning to Rick echoes Calypso's warning to Odysseus; his callous disregard for the travelers resembles the Graeae's contempt for Perseus until he steals their eye. His computer-graphic recreation of his wife's death recalls Prospero's "insubstantial pageant," and his desire for his own death evokes the Cumaean Sibyl's lament in Petronius' *Satyricon*. The scenes of Rick's party showering recall the cave's watery nature in the tales of Bucur, Mímir, and Montesinos; the banquet scene (with its plentiful wine that helps unleash Shane's rapacity) evokes the Venusberg, where Venus ruled over a continuous revel of gluttony and lust.

In Quixotic fashion, Jenner (as Montesinos) and his dead wife, or TS-19 (as the "testifying dead" Durandarte), reveal nothing but doubt and contradiction to Rick and the questers: "You have no idea what it is, do you?" they ask. He responds, "It could be microbial, viral, parasitic, fungal . . ." This doubt, the despair at the heart of the CDC bunker, is the despair of the women turned to stone in Bucur's cavern and those turned to water in Cervantes' Cave of Montesinos. It is Odysseus sobbing in homesickness on Calypso's beach and the Witch of Wookey Hole destroying love. Despair lies at the heart of every Enchanter who foresees inevitable fate, from Merlin to Mímir to the Sibyl. Jenner uses that despair as a weapon, revealing Rick's doubts to the group and advocating surrender to fiery death by HIT: "No pain. An end to sorrow, grief, regret. Everything." His spell ensnares Jacqui and almost captures Andrea—again, the predatory Enchanter peeks out.

WHAT THE ENCHANTER WHISPERS

But if *The Walking Dead* is modern myth, and Jenner is that myth's Enchanter, why is there an Enchanter in the TV show and not in the comic? This might be a function of the medium: television has less space to tell a story than a graphic novel, so any shorthand, from dramatic music to archetypal (or stereotypical; right, T-Dog?) characters, becomes essential. If archetypes actually exist in any meaningful sense, or even if they're simply societal creations, they emerge more clearly in collaborative art forms, such as ongoing television series or cycles of medieval romances, than in narratives produced by a single author, such as a novel or comics script. It might be a function of artistic design: perhaps Frank Darabont thinks in archetypal terms, while Robert Kirkman has other plans for his story.

It is perhaps significant that the potential Enchanter candidates in Kirkman's graphic novels deliberately controvert or subvert their archetypal status. Hershel Greene (appearing in issues 10–48) is more fertility priest than isolated Enchanter; it's his connections to agriculture and community that resonate in the comics, not his meager scientific arts. And if Eugene

Porter, introduced in issue fifty-three, is Merlin, he's the imposter Merlin from Mark Twain's *A Connecticut Yankee in King Arthur's Court*; his companion, the radio, proves literally hollow and empty, at least of batteries. Given the larger themes of the comics, perhaps the absence of an archetype is itself a form of archetypal criticism; having no Enchanter means that the characters in the graphic novels have no inevitable fate.

Or perhaps it's the inevitable fate of postmodern archetypes to evade their roles. Jenner himself subverts his archetypal status when he claims to be nothing but a glorified lab assistant. His wife, he says, was the real genius. If she was the Enchanter, however, her magic failed: her magnificent, glowing brain turned angry red in Vai's imagery just as quickly as any mortal's. Jenner can answer no new questions about the virus; all his data only confirm what Rick and the rest of the travelers already knew. His experiments provide no Tarnhelm, no magic cure. In *The Walking Dead*, the Enchanter's secret may well be that there is no Enchanter.

On the other hand, Jenner definitely reveals something to Rick in his whisper at the end of episode six ("TS-19"). But we don't know what it is, and by the time we do know, it won't be a revelation but a confirmation of something on the screen. Whether the Enchanter has given Rick good advice or bad news, he hasn't given it to us. Jenner is indeed a postmodern Merlin, encompassing and undermining the Enchanter archetype at the same time. Like Merlin, he's trapped in the past—the dead past that Rick is so determined to walk away from. In spite of Jenner's failure and despair—or perhaps *because* of it, reinforced by the HIT—Rick gains the courage to leave the cave and, as the mythic lesson teaches, "finally start living."

KENNETH HITE has designed, written, or co-authored more than seventy roleplaying games and supplements, including the *Star Trek Roleplaying Game*, *Day After Ragnarok*, *Trail of Cthulhu*, and *Night's Black Agents*. Outside gaming, his works include *Zombies 101*, *Tour de Lovecraft: The Tales*, *Cthulhu 101*, *Where the Deep Ones Are*, and the graphic illustrated version of *The Complete Idiot's Guide to U.S. History*. He writes the "Lost in Lovecraft" column for *Weird Tales*, and his essays and criticism have also appeared in *Dragon Magazine*, *National Review*, *Amazing Stories*, and in anthologies from Greenwood Press and MIT Press. He lives in Chicago with his wife Sheila, two cats, and many, many books. Online at princeofcairo.livejournal.com.

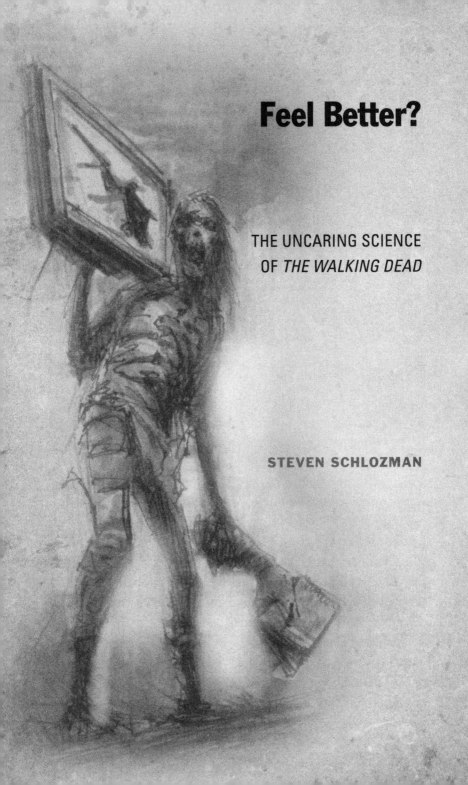

Feel Better?

THE UNCARING SCIENCE
OF *THE WALKING DEAD*

STEVEN SCHLOZMAN

Their shadows, with the magic hand of chance;
And when I feel, fair creature of an hour,
That I shall never look upon thee more,
Never have relish in the faery power
Of unreflecting love;—then on the shore
Of the wide world I stand alone, and think
Till Love and Fame to nothingness do sink.

—John Keats,
purportedly written in the midst of his fears
of dying from tuberculosis

There is a stubborn and persistent myth about science with a capital "S" that both inflames and relieves our most primal fears: *all questions will soon be answered!* This was the rallying cry about 150 years ago as society underwent powerful cultural shifts. Darwin told us about evolution in 1859. The world didn't come about in seven days. It took millions of years for life to take shape. A century before that, Linnaeus had told us that we could scientifically categorize everything that lives. The naming of the species was a function of science, not derived from the Book of Genesis. Then, around 1800, a French physician named Jean Marc Gasper Itard set out to define the human condition itself by observing the "Wild Boy of Aveyron," a feral child who was apparently raised by wolves. Science, it seemed, was promising answers to the vast unknowns of our world, and ecumenical notions slowly lost influence in popular thinking.

All this change got folks a little worked up. Whereas religion and, more broadly, faith had held sway in the human psyche's need to wonder for more than five hundred years, now, suddenly, along came biologists such as Darwin and humanists such as Itard, and the rules of what we knew, of how we knew what we knew, and perhaps most salient for the purposes of a discussion of *The Walking Dead*, of what we were comfortably letting sit in the ether of mystery radically and precipitously changed.

As it turns out, it is a surprisingly scary thing to think that you will someday have all your answers. It is also, paradoxically, a surprisingly scary thing to think that some of these answers will remain unknown. When Oscar Wilde opined that "science is the record of dead religions," there was a fair amount of anxious hand-wringing. In an era when pestilence, poverty, and brokenness surrounded anyone who walked the streets of Western modernity, the idea that science would provide solutions to all of our misery was at times little more than cold comfort. Cultural historians, in fact, suggest that the Victorian desire for rules and propriety stemmed directly from the perceived breakdown by science of previously unchallenged and religion-based worldviews.

So, what in the world does all this pontificating have to do with the science of *The Walking Dead*?

Everything.

Science, as it is often narrowly defined—that is, the cold, uncaring use of data to test and retest the informed guesses of modern hypotheses—can often be emotionally unsatisfying. Indeed, if science is our only source of solace when mystery strikes, then we must somehow improve our emotional tolerance for the uncertainty that science provides. As a species, however, we really don't *like* uncertainty. Unless we have very little to lose, we tend, adaptively, to cling to that which we know with confidence. We stay well within our comfort zone. This is where we function best.

It doesn't take a chapter in a book to tell you that the world of *The Walking Dead* is not anywhere near anyone's rational comfort zone. In the first episode of the TV series, half of what looks to have once been a woman pulls itself pitifully across the grass, its skull exposed, its eyes vacant. We do not, as a rule, have a scientific template for this kind of scenario, and the total absence of any familiarity creates intellectual and emotional dissonance. In short, our sense of horror grows precisely because we cannot explain scientifically what we are seeing.

So, as you might expect, the characters in the show and the graphic novel do exactly what the viewers and readers do. We all turn to science, with a capital "S," for answers. We listen along with Rick and his friends for reliable news, for some kind of explanation. We are therefore rapt with attention when we hear of any broadcasts leading people to believe that there might be someone out there who can offer explanation and provide assistance. After some debate, the characters decide to visit the Centers for Disease Control.

Why?

Well, the "walkers" are caused by a disease, and the CDC studies disease. No one knows more about disease than the people at the CDC. There must be armies of smart people in the government bunkers, scientists working around the clock to fix this mess. The characters take great risks, traveling into zombie-infested Atlanta, to reach the CDC headquarters. This is how far they'll go to avoid uncertainty. They'll risk life itself to escape an increasingly mangled worldview. Only the CDC can explain zombies. Add to this the unspoken recognition that answers do not necessarily provide solutions, and the tension is nearly unbearable as the final episode ("TS-19") of the first season begins.

What's the first thing we realize?

There is only one scientist. Everyone else is gone.

Okay, fine, we think. We still have faith that this one scientist will have some answers. After all, why would he be the only remaining official unless he was onto something helpful. What will the *sole scientist left in the world* tell us? Can he put an end to this chaos? *Can he help the world make sense again?*

He tries, but few people find comfort in what Dr. Edwin Jenner is able to explain.

Dr. Jenner's answers are particularly chilling precisely because they mirror so closely the similarly authoritative pronouncements that we heard and read about the SARS virus in 2003, the ongoing concerns regarding the H1N1 influenza pandemic, and even the unexplained emergence of mad cow disease. We attempt to use science to demystify and to de-horrify, but inevitably we can find both the presence and absence of scientific explanation incredibly frightening.

So, before we get into the science of the contagion that reanimates the walkers in *The Walking Dead*, ask yourself a question. When the CDC writes on its online FAQ page that "SARS is caused by a previously unrecognized coronavirus, called SARS-associated coronavirus (SARS-CoV)," and then further notes that "it is possible that other infectious agents might have a role in some cases of SARS," how much better do you feel about a scary-as-hell respiratory infection that for unclear reasons invaded major cities in Asia and then went and chose Toronto to pick on as well? You have the name of the bug—SARS, or severe acute respiratory syndrome. You know it's a coronavirus because it looks like it wears a crown—a "corona"—when you look at it under a microscope. You know that "other infectious agents" might play a role.

Feel better? Probably not, because you also know that the bug seemed to come out of nowhere. It managed to disrupt everything from international travel to (*gasp!*) Major League Baseball, and many people perished before the virus slipped out of our world again and back into our nightmares. The SARS scare now lurks in our memories, reminding us that every mild upper respiratory infection, the usual symptoms of the 10 zillion coronaviruses that make us moderately miserable every year, has the potential to be something different, something new, something deadly, that we can define and categorize but that we can't do a damn thing about. Think about that the next time somebody sneezes on you in an airport.

Now, suddenly, those stuffy Victorians seem more like scared rats, trying to make sense of a sudden change in their very way of thinking about the world. You cannot have science, and especially the rules of science alone, without sacrificing some kind of certainty. The Black Death of the fourteenth century was at the time largely attributed to divine wrath. One cannot question divine wrath because it is, by definition, a faith-based conclusion. You "believe" in it. It does not require the tests of science. However, the Age of Reason, the birth of modern science, called for all things unexplained to be solved through scientific inquiry. With regard to infectious agents like the SARS virus, science answers some of our questions but remains stubbornly ignorant as well. Anyone want some Purell?

Now that we've all appropriately got the willies, let's think a bit about what Dr. Jenner says as he is staring at the giant monitor and watching again the demise of what we later learn was his beloved and brilliant wife.

"It could be microbial, viral, parasitic, fungal."

Well, that narrows it down.

It is notable as well that it is this apparently dry scientific pronouncement that unleashes a fresh burst of abject horror. Jenner essentially runs the gamut of every infectious agent that harbors an affinity for human hosts. By rattling off all that he knows in the absence of a solid or satisfying answer, he plunges the viewer and the characters on the show into the greatest uncertainty they have yet to face.

To be fair, we can make a few assumptions from what we've already seen. We know the bug appears to be transmitted through bodily fluids. We know it doesn't seem to be airborne, or our characters would be sick. We know it triggers an immune response because its victims develop a fever. And we know that it is highly efficient; so far, everyone who was bitten has changed. We also know that the bug has found a great means of propagating itself. Scary bugs like Ebola burn themselves out—the victims die horribly and so quickly that they don't have time to "help" the virus to transmit itself to other victims. The walkers continue to walk, and anything living they encounter is fair game for furthering the infection's progress.

If the learned man, the scientist—the freakin' CDC, for goodness' sake—can't narrow it down any more than to list every infectious agent on Earth, then we are in much deeper trouble than we had previously imagined. Saying what we *do* know is the backward way Jenner expresses all that we do not. It wouldn't surprise the Victorians one bit that Jenner agrees with another survivor's suggestion that it could also be "an act of God." At that point, he has thrown in the scientific towel entirely, because he abandons the guiding principles of science that have presumably governed his intellectual and professional life to date. And this is the CDC! Time to get out, Rick notes. Nothing more to see here.

The science of *The Walking Dead* takes our terror further than Ebola can take us, further than nuclear war can take us, further than some of our most cherished science fiction. Ripley at least knows what she's dealing with in *Aliens*. "Get away from her, you bitch!" she screams, and the alien really is sort of a bitch. In *The Walking Dead*, we can't even narrow down the contagion to the most basic classification of pathogens. We can't call it a bitch or a monster or really anything other than bad luck. And we humans don't like it much when we are prevented from assigning to our adversaries attributes at least minimally related to ourselves.

As if to accentuate the point, Jenner walks us all through the progression of the disease. Using an MRI of the brain—an "extraordinary brain," Jenner tells us—he starts by showing us the endless connections and interconnections of neurons that make us human. Remember, the brain has about 100 million neurons and 100 trillion connections. To say that it is a giant computer is unfair to the mass of goo that sits packed tightly in our cranial cavity; computers don't stand a chance against our gray matter. Let's consider for a moment Jenner's brief description of the brain's inner workings.

Imagine that you wake up and find yourself wanting coffee. That simple realization is immensely complex and synergistic. Literally tens of thousands of neurons in your prefrontal cortex dimly remember that coffee makes things seem a bit clearer. But the "remembering" comes from the other regions of the brain— the hippocampus, for example, and the dopamine reward centers that are eager to taste again what is, after all, a fairly addictive substance. You then realize that you can already smell that coffee, that your loved one is in the kitchen and has already got the pot brewing. It smells good, and the olfactory bulb, sitting, as it does, so near the centers for neurobiological memory, kicks the thought of your loved one making coffee to the higher cortical regions, where you feel a happy desire to wait in bed a bit longer to see if he or she will bring the coffee directly to you. He or she used to do that all the time, but ever since the baby was born, it happens as a rare treat, and thus the meaning of that action—the neocortical understanding of what it means to share love, for example—has changed in the last few months.

You move a bit in bed, and your back hurts. The somatosensory cortex notes this and posits the reasons to your frontal lobe that your back doesn't feel right. There might be a fleeting recollection of the last time your back hurt, and you might recall that it bought you a few days home without work. Because you are an adult, you have the capacity, based on the density and connectivity of the neurons in your frontal lobe, to indulge in the simultaneous experience of competing desires in which you dread another episode of lower back pain but recall fondly lying in bed all day the last time it happened and watching again every episode of *Firefly*.

All the while, your brain stem reminds your heart to beat and your lungs to breathe, and you are vaguely aware by signals sent from the detrusor muscles in your bladder back into that web of tangled signals in your head that you have to pee. And having to pee makes you remember that time you were stuck on a plane with a full bladder and sitting in the window seat next to a woman whose child was finally sleeping peacefully on her mother's breast.

All these thoughts, what Freud called "associations," what he and others attribute to the associative properties of the human brain, are what make us uniquely human. Someone else might wake up and want tea, or be horribly hungover and desire nothing more than for the throbbing headache to stop, or want to linger in bed and savor thoughts of the previous night's date.

As the poet in Dr. Jenner tells us, all those "ripples of light" on the screen are "you." Uniquely you.

This is what Jenner is getting at when he talks of "the extinction event." The humanoid creatures wandering the face of the Earth outside the CDC walls can't make those associations or experience those fond memories of love and hate. They can't be human, and humans are therefore on their way out, because no one, not even the French, Jenner tells us, has the slightest idea what the hell caused this mess.

So, when the brain on Jenner's monitor moves through its seminal events, we see immense complexity and then a stark absence—death—of the very complexity that we just a second before celebrated. Then we watch with dread "the resurrection event," in which nothing but the basest of neurobiological drives is displayed electronically on the CDC Jumbotron. The heart beats, the lungs breathe, and the mouth feeds. When Rick asks if what he sees on the screen is alive, Jenner's voice grows even more monotone. "You tell me," he says.

This is the crux of the terror. The walkers, the zombies, the resurrected individuals, are "shells," totally impersonal, completely without desires or passions, happiness or misery. We don't define human life by a beating heart; we define it by what that heart—or, less poetically but more scientifically accurate, that brain—desires. In the absence of individuality there is an absence of humanity. What makes us human is our capacity to be uniquely individual pack animals. In *The Walking Dead*, what takes that humanity away is the abolition of the individual. None of those living dead things will fall in love or write poetry. They are, for all intents and purposes, walking manifestations of disease. The walkers exist only to propagate the contagion within. You can't really hate them, precisely because they lack the capacity to hate you back. Nothing bugs us more than a lack of personal investment. If something is going to end our lives, end our very reasons for being, we'd like that something to be specifically and individually about us. About Shane, or Lori, or Dale, or Rick. The fact that a walker will just as readily attack one person as another foils our attempts to understand why some get sick and some do not. The scientist in us knows that contagions don't really care as long as the infrastructure is there. Contagions are squatters. They'll take what they can get. But the more primitive parts of our psyche, the places we go when the unexpected and unfair occurs, want badly to have reasons for things. The walkers, or more appropriately, the infection itself, take away all reason. *That is scary as hell.*

Why, then, we might ask, do the characters of *The Walking Dead* cling to their seemingly insignificant and clearly maladaptive systems of belief? Why make enemies of each other when facing an extinction event? Why beat the hell out of one of the few remaining humans? Don't we need one another to survive? We can use the most cutting-edge neurobiology to address these questions; however, as is often the case with science, the answers might not be particularly satisfying.

Mirror neuron theory is essentially a neurobiological model for empathy. A monkey, when shown another monkey in pain, will recruit regions of its own brain that correlate with the suffering monkey's pain. In other words, one monkey feels what another monkey experiences and, in so doing, feels for the monkey with exactly the same regions of the brain that are activated in the monkey feeling directly inflicted pain. The experiment need not be this nefarious. The same findings occur in monkeys and humans when the monkeys or humans watch others having a good time. Watching someone taste something sweet triggers in the watcher's brain regions that are associated not only with envy or thirst but also with taste. We are wired to connect with each other, and our brains seem to crave and enjoy the experience of knowing and biologically replicating what others are up to.

Not so with zombies. You can shoot a zombie, and it doesn't care. You can bash in the skull of what used to be a zombie's wife, and it doesn't care. The brain scans that Jenner shows us suggest that whatever regions might have been activated via mirror neurons when humans weren't infected are now completely gone in the walkers. There is neither empathy nor wrath among the adversaries of those who survive the zombie apocalypse.

So what do we do? We take all that wrath, all that emotion that we'd expect back from something that appears to hate us so much that it would eviscerate us without a second thought, and we direct it toward one another. The zombies aren't mad at us. *They couldn't care less* about our uniquely personal attributes. Your guts are as satisfying as the person's next to you, and we therefore have an uncaring, unfeeling enemy. Compare this to the acid-blood beast in the *Alien* movies. That thing seems to personally hate Ripley, and she hates it right back.

But remember the first episode of *The Walking Dead*. Remember Morgan's undead wife? Rick looks at her through the peephole of the door, and he struggles mightily, millions of neurons in his still-human brain trying to reconcile what is outside the door with what used to be Morgan's wife. But the zombie? She just stares. *There is nothing there but a zombie.* Her brain is gone, and so she is gone as well. She exists only to feed.

Max Brooks made this point clear in *World War Z*. In the fabulous and ominous description of the battle of Yonkers, the narrator recalls throwing every sort of weapon he has at the horde of zombies. What he sees scares him more than anything he has seen to date: "Shock and Awe!" he exclaims. "But what if the enemy can't be shocked and awed? Not just won't, but biologically *can't*!"

Microbes, viruses, parasites, and funguses can't be awed. They are biologically incapable of shock or fear. And in Brooks' story, as in *The Walking Dead* and every good zombie movie for that matter, all that expelled wrath bounces back and ricochets throughout the remaining motley crew of survivors. Things get worse, not better, because unlike previous enemies, these adversaries can't be demonized. The zombies lack all personal attributes.

But despite all these dour observations, you have to admit that the science of the twenty-first century has been uniquely personal and absolutely astounding. We've seen photographs of Martian sunsets. We've watched primates control mechanical arms with their thoughts. The average life span of someone in the West with HIV/AIDS is now more than five times what it was as recently as thirty years ago. You'd have to be emotionally blind to miss the wonders that science has brought us.

Nonetheless, science can also leave us cold and empty. The current fascination with apocalyptic scenarios is evidence that we take this science with a grain of proverbial salt.

"This is what takes us down," Jenner says. "This is our extinction event." He makes a reasonable prediction based on scientific inquiry, and yet this is hardly a warm, fuzzy moment. In fact, the whole damn CDC building is blown to smithereens just as the season concludes.

This is the best that science can offer. Feel better?

STEVEN SCHLOZMAN is the author of *The Zombie Autopsies: Secret Notebooks from the Apocalypse*. He has lectured about zombie neuroscience for the National Academy of Sciences, medical schools, and the American

Psychiatric Association. Schlozman has appeared with George Romero discussing horror genre films. He has written about psychiatry and child psychiatry for ABC, *USA Today*, and *Newsweek*, and about popular culture for *Psychology Today* and *The Boston Globe*. He earned his MD from Brown University in 1994 and trained in psychiatry and child psychiatry at Harvard Medical School, where he is currently an assistant professor. He also serves as a staff physician at Massachusetts General Hospital and the co-director of medical student education in psychiatry at Harvard University. Online at thezombieautopsies.com.

The Walking Dead and Dance of Death

OR, WHY THE ZOMBIES ARE ALWAYS ON THE OTHER SIDE OF THE FENCE

LISA MORTON

S ee if this sounds familiar: A skillfully rendered sequence of black-and-white drawings tells the tale of everyday people caught in the middle of a plague, surrounded on all sides by skeletal, undead monsters. This work has become famous, has influenced other artists, and has been reprinted in a variety of different editions.

Now, imagine it's nearly five hundred years old.

Long before the dead shambled in comics such as Robert Kirkman's *The Walking Dead*, they danced in a series of forty-one engravings by the artist Hans Holbein the Younger. First published in 1538, Holbein's *Dance of Death* was a response to a world ravaged by the Black Death, and in Holbein's art, Death is a living figure, depicted in each engraving interacting with a different member of society. Death appears as a skeleton, sometimes with a few tattered shreds of skin draped over his rib cage, and often mocking his victims by wearing their clothing. For example, in "The Child," Death wears a peasant's cap and drags an innocent toddler out of his home while mother and sibling look on in horror. No one escaped Death's clutches—Holbein shows everyone from a queen to a ploughman to a robber being taken by his Grim Reaper. Holbein's interest in the Plague was borne out by his own death, since many scholars believe he succumbed to the disease in 1543.

Holbein may have been known in his time as a painter and for his work as the official artist at the court of Henry VIII, but he's

THE CHILD

now remembered mainly for the striking and gruesome *Dance of Death* series. Though it's difficult to trace a direct connection to Holbein, modern horror comics certainly derive from the same tradition. You can see Holbein's leering, skeletal Death in EC's Crypt-Keeper of the 1950s or the Warren comics hosts of the 1960s such as Uncle Creepy. Later dark fantasy comics such as Neil Gaiman's *Sandman* sometimes depicted Death as a character interacting with everyday life, and the stark, expressionistic black-and-white art by Eddie Campbell for Alan Moore's *From Hell* almost emulates wood engravings. Perhaps no other graphic novel or comic illustration has come as close to Holbein's disturbing images of a world in the grip of plague and death as *The Walking Dead*. However, despite the similarities, the differences between the two works are ultimately more interesting. Even though Holbein's creation may have been an early precursor to the work of Robert Kirkman, Charlie Adlard, Tony Moore, and Cliff Rathburn, the use of space and distance to show the proximity of death couldn't be more different between *Dance of Death* and *The Walking Dead*, and these dissimilarities and contrasts cast in a dark light the times and cultures in which the works were created.

In Kirkman's script for *The Walking Dead*, a global plague has resulted in zombies—resurrected corpses that feed on the living. Our protagonist, Rick Grimes, is a small-town police officer who, at the beginning of the story, is injured in a gunfight and slips into a coma for an undefined number of days. Rick awakens in an abandoned hospital and finds his family and other survivors near Atlanta, and together they set off in search of sanctuary. Along the way, they encounter a gated community, a protected farm, a prison, and finally a town set up by the government in case of a holocaust. Their group acquires a former pro football player, a college student, a gym teacher, a pizza delivery boy (who was also an occasional car thief), a congressman, and a lawyer, and they confront outlaws, pirates, dictators, and—most often—zombies. Nowhere in this brave new world is safe; zombies lurk in the cities, the small towns, the houses, the shops, the streets, and the woods. The survivors' first consideration upon encountering a possible new settlement is protection from the "roamers." Zombies control their lives, their movements, their entire existence.

Given the overwhelming presence of zombies and how intrinsic they are to every turn of the plot in *The Walking Dead*, a reader would expect to see panel after panel showing the dead and the living side by side, in close juxtaposition.

But this isn't 1538; death is not a nearby, familiar guide leading the way to the end in *The Walking Dead*, and the art often emphasizes a distance between the roamers and the human protagonists. "We're *surrounded* by death. It's taken over our *lives*," former file clerk Andrea complains in one scene, which takes place in a farmyard surrounded by a fence high enough to keep out zombies. The implication is that even though *The Walking Dead*'s characters recognize death's ubiquity, they still strive to keep it physically distant. Compare *The Walking Dead*'s farm scene, in which Andrea stands in a carefully fenced-off yard, with no zombies visible, to Holbein's engraving of "The Ploughman," in which Death works alongside a farmer who is tilling the soil. In fact, Holbein occasionally shows Death as a friendly or even helpful presence: he leads "The Blind Man" over rocks, entertains "The New-Married Lady" with a drum performance, and joins "The Idiot Fool" in a gleeful jig.

Throughout the *Walking Dead* comics, the survivors are placed behind bars, walls, fences, or trees; in vehicles; or on rooftops. Zombies—if they're shown at all—often appear separated by either a physical barrier or space. The zombies are occasionally further separated by the use of a different art style—a gray wash is applied to a crowd of zombies, for example, rendering them as one grim mass and also completely distinguishing them from the carefully delineated humans. In one of the more striking depictions of this distance in the entire series, in the story arc titled "Too Far Gone," Glenn, a former pizza delivery man, and Heath, a dreadlocked runner, leave the safety of the protected community and venture into the nearby city in search of antibiotics, only to have their way unexpectedly blocked by zombies. In a two-page tableau, the two men stare down from the top of a tall building into a narrow alley packed with the dead. "Not clear," Heath notes and then adds, "Not even close."

But the story arc involving the prison provides the most distinctive visual depictions of separation and distance. Charlie Adlard's art makes a prison—surely the most claustrophobic of structures—into a welcoming vista of wide-open spaces, carefully separated from the outside world by three layers of fences.

A telling cover graces issue forty-one: Rick on one side of the prison's chain-link fence and a female zombie, her face hidden by hair, making her faceless, on the other. Interestingly, this issue centers in part on that zombie, taken in by medical student Alice as a sort of experiment, yet the cover renders the zombie in complete separation. In a two-page interior sequence, a zombie is stabbed in the head by a knife thrust through the prison's outer fence, but the zombie and the knife wielder, Glenn, are never shown in the same panel. The living Glenn is completely separated from death, even when he's the one delivering it.

It isn't the art alone in *The Walking Dead* that emphasizes how death and life exist separately from each other. Robert Kirkman's scripts also hammer the idea home from issue to issue. The characters occasionally admit their denial openly: "I've seen *too much* death," Rick's wife, Lori, grouses at one point; later on, when former convict Axel brings up a question about the zombies, down-to-earth farmer Hershel tells him, "I try not to think about *them* at all." Both Lori's and Hershel's comments suggest that they are clinging to a former way of life in which death was rarely seen; neither is acknowledging that death is now and will continue to be ubiquitous.

These exchanges both occur in a prison yard that Rick's people are converting into a vegetable field, and of course, no zombies are visible in either scene. The survivors in *The Walking Dead* are, in fact, so anxious to separate themselves from death that a prison looks idyllic to them. Indeed, the prison remains the one location where the comics, in the first eighty or so issues, have spent the longest amount of time, and the script makes rich (and even funny) use of the notion of prison as ultimate barrier. As they first enter the dank and bloodied but zombie-free cell block, former pro athlete Tyreese says, "Man, *Rick* . . . this is *nice*." Compare that to second-in-command Abraham's first words when they walk into a (seemingly) functional suburban community, the Alexandria Safe-Zone: "This is fucking *weird*." Abraham, as it turns out, is absolutely right—the wide-open suburban streets *are* fucking weird, and his recognition of the seeming absence of death marks him as a realist and keeps him alive. Likewise, Michonne's entrance into the series marks her as a survivor: she appears outside the prison walls casually striding through a mass of zombies, disguised by two chained zombies that accompany her. Michonne, a former lawyer who happens to be good with a sword, is thus introduced as someone who is literally willing to walk side by side with death. Lori, Hershel, and Tyreese, however, are doomed by their failure to accept this new world. Their denial of death is exactly what will lead to their own undeniable deaths.

The ironic aspect of life within prison walls is intensified by a moment when Rick, faced with what he believes to be a naïve point of view expressed by several of those he's leading, has an outburst: "We're *surrounded* by the *dead*. We're *among* them—and when we finally give up, *we become them*! [. . .] You think we hide behind walls to protect us from *the walking dead*! Don't you *get it*? We *are* the walking dead!" As he utters the final sentence, we get a two-page close-up of Rick, his face so bruised and battered from a recent fistfight that he does indeed bear a resemblance to the zombies whom we glimpse, throughout the speech, through a chain-link fence, the frames slowly bringing them in closer. Rick seems to be moving toward an acceptance of death; like Holbein's "Blind Man," he's walking with Death now.

Yet Rick's revelation only serves to allow the characters to act with more open savagery. Not long after this, the psychotic character the Governor is introduced, and the series steps briefly away from the zombies to focus on the intense and startlingly gruesome human-on-human violence committed both by and on the Governor. Death continues to surround *The Walking Dead*'s characters, but now they have become both the engine of death and the victim. Holbein, again, was right: death is ever present and must be accepted.

Early on in the series, after Rick has found the encampment where Lori and their son, Carl, are living with other survivors, we see another variation on living with death. Rick decides that they need more guns, and more guns can only be obtained by venturing into Atlanta, which has been overrun by the dead. Rick, looking for a way to disguise himself, discovers that the living can blend in with the zombies and move undetected among them by covering themselves with "roamer" blood and body parts. Unfortunately, Rick's plan nearly proves lethal when rain washes the disguising scent away, but the plan is still effective enough to allow him to return to the encampment with guns. This method would logically have been completely successful had it not been for the rain, and is shown in one later issue to work until two new members of Rick's group panic, revealing their humanity. To blend in with the zombies—to move freely among the dead and thus to fully accept death—is not a habit the living are willing to adopt.

Obviously, living beneath a blanket of zombie guts isn't a pleasant option (even on sunny days), but there are situations, like the aforementioned trip into a city for antibiotics, when it would seem to offer a viable alternative to the dangers of leaping from buildings to avoid hungry "biters." Why, then, wouldn't our protagonists avail themselves of this useful subterfuge?

The answer can be found in part by contrasting the survivors with the characters of Holbein's *Dance*. For instance, in his engraving of "The Countess," as the wealthy older woman dresses, assisted by a servant, Death also helps, offering her almost a loving embrace, bony arms wrapped around her shoulders. Holbein is telling us that

THE COUNTESS

even a wealthy countess must succumb, but she seems accepting of this, showing no fear or dismay at the touch of Death.

The characters of *The Walking Dead*, however, are not medieval Europeans but contemporary Americans. Before the zombie outbreak, even Rick—the cop who was almost mortally wounded—wasn't used to death. Early in the first issue of the comic, Rick encounters his first desiccated corpse, this one truly dead, as it falls out of an opening elevator, and the expression of horror on his face tells us this is not a man inured to death. In fact, in a November 1, 2010, interview with *Entertainment Weekly*, Kirkman described Rick this way: "Rick Grimes was not a police officer that had used his gun very often. He was just one of those guys that basically just walks by the local malt shop and made sure the kids were getting home on time."

Rick, like most of the characters in *The Walking Dead*, is a typical modern Westerner, and as such lives much of his life in denial of death. The industrial revolution urbanized the landscape in the nineteenth century and removed most workers from the everyday encounters with death experienced in farms and villages. Meat became a product, and consumers seldom related it to the slaying of an animal; the housewife purchasing a clean pork loin from the neighborhood butcher was removed from the killing of the pig. By 1906, France had attempted to abolish the death penalty, and in America, burials no longer took place on family property. Midway through the twentieth century, death was so far removed from the average person's life that a book like Jessica Mitford's 1963 exposé on the funeral industry, *The American Way of Death*, was a must-read bestseller as much for its shock value as its journalistic excellence. Mitford's editors apparently even initially requested that she remove the detailed chapter on embalming, which they considered to be too disturbing.

Fortunately for horror fans, Mitford's publishers aren't putting out *The Walking Dead*, and there's certainly plenty of blood to be found in the comic's pages. Of course, by the time *The Walking Dead* debuted as a monthly comic in 2003, the modern zombie was well established, and no self-respecting zombie chronicler would dream of producing a movie, novel, game, or comic that didn't include at least a few scenes of graphic cannibalism, dismemberment, and other forms of mutilation. Yet, strangely enough, even some of the most gruesome scenes in *The Walking Dead* are distanced from the human protagonists. *The Walking Dead*'s creators know we want to test our limits, to experience the violent side effects of death, even while living in denial of it. The first two sequences to present zombies in the act of eating are an example. The first one comes when Rick has ridden a horse into Atlanta, and a horde of undead attackers separate him from his mount and feast on the horse, which is shown in a single panel full of zombies and horse guts. The second scene involves Rick and his partner, Shane, tracking a deer in the woods. They find that a zombie has beaten them to their quarry, and once again, the monstrous meal is presented in a single frame with an emphasis on the blood. The next panel shows Rick and Shane reacting in dismay, and the dialogue— "Do you think it'd be safe to eat?"—suggests that they are not frightened of the zombie but rather upset that it has taken their prey. As with Holbein's art, death is a part of the natural order here—even if Rick's reaction to seeing the zombie eating the deer tells us that he hasn't yet transformed into the man who accepts that he is one of the walking dead.

While it's tempting to suggest that this inverse "we are the predator but we deny death" formula might be at the heart of all zombie tales, *The Walking Dead* ultimately delivers a more complicated—and more optimistic—message. Children are featured in both Holbein's art and *The Walking Dead*, and in both works, children are the ultimate victims. In Holbein's "The Child"—considered by many historians to be the most horrifying of all the engravings—a youngster is yanked cruelly away from his helpless, wailing family. Rick's young son, Carl, on the other hand, may have barely survived so far, but he's painfully aware of the constant threat and of how little truly separates the mortals from their doom. When Rick and the others find the protected suburban enclave just outside of Washington, D.C., it's little Carl who has the hardest time adjusting to a life that seems secure and peaceful. When Rick asks his son why he's not enjoying Halloween trick-or-treat activities with the other kids, Carl notes that "the roamers don't go away because you can't *see* them." Allen, one of the more sensitive—and sensible— adults in the first half of the series, tries to teach his two young sons about the dangers of denying death: "Death is a part of your *lives* now [. . .] We're *all* going to die. We have to get used to that. We have to be *okay* with that—we have to *expect* it, *welcome* it. Because if we don't—it will hurt us . . . *a lot.* And you don't want it to *hurt.*" The younger characters seem to be fully aware of how close to death they truly are, and this gives *The Walking Dead* an odd sense of hope. As civilization fades, the humans who will survive in this new world are the ones who encapsulate the values of the old, preindustrial world. Those who accept death—like Carl, Abraham, Michonne, and Rick— will live on in the knowledge that someday Death will walk past the fence, extend a hand, and ask them to dance. Holbein would undoubtedly approve.

LISA MORTON is a screenwriter and the author of four books of nonfiction, including *The Halloween Encyclopedia*, recently released in a second edition. Her short fiction has been published in numerous books and magazines; recent appearances include *The Mammoth Book of Zombie Apocalypse!* and *The Dead That Walk.* Lisa is a four-time Bram Stoker Award winner, having most recently received the 2010 First Novel award for *The Castle of Los Angeles.* She is also a renowned expert on Halloween who has appeared on the History Channel and in the pages of *The Wall Street Journal.* She lives in North Hollywood, California. Online at lisamorton.com.

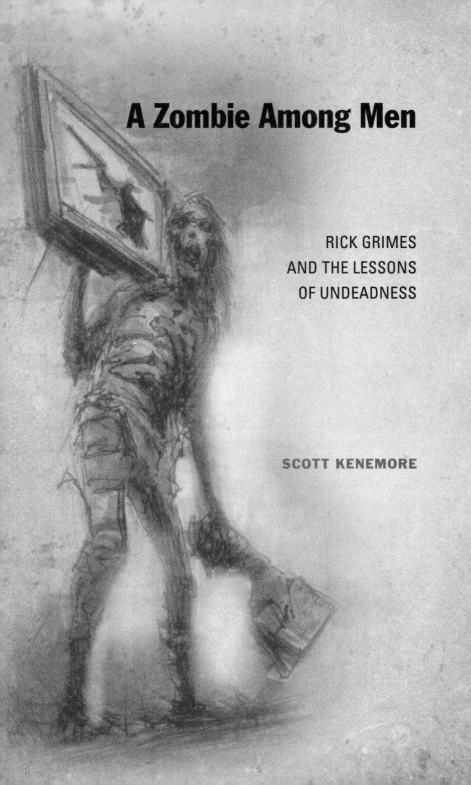

A Zombie Among Men

RICK GRIMES
AND THE LESSONS
OF UNDEADNESS

SCOTT KENEMORE

Robert Kirkman's epic comic book series is called *The Walking Dead*.

Not *The Whiny Humans*.

Can we agree on that much? Can we all accept that this, at least, is fact and not just "my opinion"?

Can we?

Good.

Because there's a reason he gave it that title.

Kirkman's phenomenal series makes perhaps the strongest case in contemporary fiction for the superiority of the zombie over the human. It is on the positive traits of zombies that Kirkman has chosen to focus his narrative, and rightly so. In the dark and apocalyptic world of *The Walking Dead*—so expertly limned by Kirkman—it is the zombies and not the humans who consistently find ways to persevere, who succeed, eventually, in obtaining their goals. Wherever they are and whatever they are doing, zombies always have the advantage. They triumph where humans fail. They endure in situations that would leave living persons totally obliterated. These dynamic, ever-stalwart, and supremely self-assured wonders are an inspiration to us all—but never more than to Kirkman's own characters.

I could, if I so wished (and if space would allow), make this point by producing a litany of instances in which capable, strong, and resourceful human characters are bitten, killed, or otherwise defeated by zombies. *The Walking Dead* provides no shortage of illustrative examples. Time after time, the zombies prevail and feed while the humans die, flee, or fight each other.

Yet it is not this consistent tactical dominance that provides the most persuasive evidence for the superiority of the zombie over the human in Kirkman's world. Rather, it is the way Kirkman's humans—however ineluctably—come to the realization that to survive a zombie apocalypse, they must *become like zombies themselves*. No one comes to understand this better than the central protagonist of the comic book series.

The Walking Dead begins by introducing us to Rick Grimes, the primary and longest-surviving member of the cast. (At the time of this writing, Kirkman is still adding to *The Walking Dead*, but there is every reason to believe this will continue to be true.) So why does Rick enjoy such longevity? Outwardly, he seems bereft of special talents. We know little more than that he is a police officer, originally from rural Kentucky. There is never any reference to a college education. There is no evidence provided that he has had military training or knows special survival skills. While it is reasonable to assume that Rick has at least a rudimentary familiarity with firearms because of his job, he is certainly no master at combat. Michonne's exemplary sword-fighting skills far exceed Rick's meager abilities with weapons. The ex-football player Tyreese is a superior physical specimen to Rick in every way and consequently has greater hand-to-hand fighting skills. And though it feels in bad taste to note, one cannot forget that Rick finds himself waking up in an abandoned hospital at the beginning of the series *because he lost a gunfight and got shot*. Simply put, he lacked the superior aim and sharp eye necessary to bring down his opponent first.

But Rick survives in a world of zombies, while others—who appear to possess more enviable skill sets—do not.

Indeed, in situation after situation, Rick survives. Surviving becomes what he does. He avoids death, evades capture, and kills those who would kill him, establishing himself as a natural leader. Rick becomes the kind of person to whom others turn for advice and counsel in a world gone mad and filled with zombies. How does he do this? *By being like a zombie.*

Rick shows that even in an apocalypse, there is hope for all of us—or at least those of us willing to learn. Learning, you see, is the key. Rick himself is no natural zombie. Rather, the zomboid traits that allow him to survive are something he picks up as he goes along.

Rick's first encounter with a zombie does not go well—to put it gently. Disoriented and confused after his convalescence, Rick enters a hospital cafeteria filled with the walking dead. The nearest zombie lumbers forward, accosting him. As Rick retreats in cowardly terror, he tries to reason with the zombie, at one point crying, "Can't you *understand*?!"

Of course, the zombie cannot understand. It attacks Rick without hesitation or regard for his words. Rick flees and lives to fight another day, but to his credit, he learns from this encounter. In a zombie world, words don't matter. Actions do. Yes, there are auditory communications of a sort between humans and zombies, but they are never so nuanced as to involve the meaning of words. Noise—be it human voices, firearm discharges, or the hum of an automobile's engine—has the power to draw the attention of zombies. In the world of *The Walking Dead*, human-made sound just communicates, "Hey, big boy, look over here."

Then Rick lets us down. As he leaves the hospital and begins to explore the interesting and exciting zombie world around him, readers are treated to pages of soliloquy in which Rick feels sad and confused and wonders what happened to his family.

I know, right? Snooze city.

But it's important that we meet Rick Version 1.0 so that we appreciate his remarkable transformation into a non-whiny, ass-kicking dynamo who is very like a zombie.

Rick continues to learn. By the time he wanders into downtown Atlanta, he is resolute and violent. When he encounters zombies, he—like a zombie—refrains from engaging his targets in conversation. He simply attacks or runs. There is nothing else to do. There is certainly no use for discourse.

When Rick reconnects with his family outside the city, he is forced to become intimately familiar with other paralyzing and inconvenient traits that make humans inferior to zombies. In this slipshod, cobbled-together version of human society (or whatever you want to call their collection of RVs parked together) Rick is thrown into a world of feelings and emotion and sexual intercourse—all things that zombies eschew completely. Rick soon discovers the reason why.

In a word, it is conflict.

Humans—unlike composed, unflappable, focused zombies—fight with one another. They are jealous. They are manipulative. They care about things like other people not having sex with their wives. And some folks continue to maintain that these humans—who can't even find the good sense to put their genitals away during a goddamn zombie apocalypse—are the superior life-forms? Seriously? Whatever, dude.

Camaraderie and teamwork do not come naturally to these humans, and they waste valuable time attempting to bond as a cohesive group—sometimes with disastrous results. Zombies, to the contrary, naturally work in unison with other zombies around them. There is no evidence that this is the result of a conscious decision to employ teamwork, but it has largely the same effect. The zombies in *The Walking Dead* distinguish between other zombies and living humans. Those in the latter category obsess them entirely. Those in the former are not worth acknowledging and certainly aren't worth fighting with.

As the humans distract themselves by reminiscing over a campfire and sharing their stories of misfortune and struggle, Rick watches a member of their party—Amy—get ambushed and brutally killed by a zombie that had all the camaraderie it ever needed the moment it rose from the grave. Rick sees this. Rick learns from it.

Over the course of several boring and emotion-filled exchanges with other humans—including his own son and wife—Rick begins to understand the way that emotions complicate survival for humans. Worrying about each other is the big one. It's something zombies just don't do. Oh sure, they often move as herds, attack as giant groups, and enjoy the benefits of strength in numbers, but all the while, they maintain an almost nonexistent regard for their fellow walking dead.

Rick also takes a step (or shamble) in the right direction when he begins to make a point of conserving resources. Zombies, of course, are consummate environmentalists, maintaining a completely organic existence. They use nothing. They produce no waste other than the 100 percent biodegradable carcasses of their kills. No part of their existence creates an environmental disturbance (except maybe to graveyard landscaping). Even as he fights for his life against zombies, Rick notices the benefits of their lack of dependence on finite resources. We see this actualized when Rick and Tyreese work together to take out roamers and opt to use hammers instead of firearms. Truly, this is the replenishable, renewable, environmentally sound option. Hammers do not use ammunition, so Rick is freed from the concern of ever finding more. Even as he lessens his environmental impact, Rick is decreasing the number of things he requires. Needing nothing at all, except fresh brains, is just one of the benefits of being a zombie.

Rick and his party meet the homesteader Hershel Greene. Though Hershel has managed to maintain a relatively safe situation on his farm, he suffers from an all-too-human failing that threatens to undermine his entire operation. Hershel has locked his infected, zombified family members in the barn next to his house and, for sentimental reasons, is unable to bring himself to shoot them through the head. The problem with this—which, to his credit, Rick immediately recognizes—is the threat to life and limb it presents. These zombie family members could escape and attack the remaining humans (which, as focused, resourceful zombies, they have every intention of doing). However, Hershel's strange need to keep his infected family around betrays a deeper, more fundamental problem.

Succinctly, Hershel is unable to accept the world for what it is. I mean, let's face it. Horrible things have happened—to the stupid humans, at least. Corpses have risen from their graves. Some of Hershel's own children have become members of the walking dead club. His former family members would just as soon bite his face off as look at him. Yet his response has not been to admit, "Well, that sucks," and to carry on. No. Instead, Hershel is stuck on the false hope that someway, somehow, his family members can be saved and their status as zombies reversed.

Dumbass.

As subsequent events make clear—through zombie carnage and mayhem—Rick is correct to conclude that Hershel's situation cannot end well. Rick also learns a valuable lesson: no matter how horrible things are in a zombie apocalypse, one *must* accept that they are real and irreversible. Zombies do this instantly. They awake from their graves into a netherworld of murder and chaos. Do they allow the oddness of this to flummox them? Do they become sad or sentimental? *Not for a moment.* They accept their situations and pop up on the hunt for brains.

Lesson learned.

Or is it?

A few pages after we're introduced to Hershel's epic self-delusions, we watch the following exchange between Rick and another survivor.

RICK: You doing okay?

ALLEN: I don't know, Rick. It's been a *while* since I had a frame of reference for *"okay."*

Here, Kirkman is firmly channeling Foucault, Sartre, and other twentieth-century existentialists to drive home another point about the superiority of zombies. Humans seek to know the unknowable so they can feel normal and healthy. Zombies do not trouble themselves with these paralyzing unknowabilities. Consequently, they are effective killers, able to survive nearly any set of difficult circumstances.

As Kirkman (and Foucault and Sartre before him) clearly understands, "normal" is an idea we invented to make ourselves feel better. Anything, at any time, can become normal if there's enough of it. Zombies—bless their nonphilosophical souls—can accept this truth instantly, without hesitation. In the world of *The Walking Dead*, humans who accept things can persevere and survive. The ones who don't usually die, often during boring, whiny soliloquies exploring how "weird" things feel now that the dead are risen. Rick instigates less existential pondering than the rest of the humans—though, alas, not none at all (which would be the perfect amount). He doubts his ability as a leader and often blames himself for tragedies that befall his band. However, his ponderings tend to be more along the lines of "Why do I suck so much?" than "Why does the world suck so much?" For Rick, it is personal and not existential.

Perhaps no sequence in *The Walking Dead* crystallizes the need for humans to be like zombies as perfectly as the period the survivors spend inside the abandoned prison. The shift from a nomadic navigation of the zombie wasteland to a stationary, fortified position—as well as the introduction of new characters to their band—forces Rick and the other humans to consider and codify their rules. They are, once again, building a little society. But as subsequent events make clear, *because it is in the midst of a zombie wasteland*, their rules will prove effective only when they direct humans to act like zombies. Their rules will prove inadequate or outright impotent when they embody human notions like "a fair trial" and "proof" and "things other than indiscriminate killing of humans."

Rick—our hero for a reason—memorably articulates his most important rule: "*You kill. You die.*" (This is the reverse of the order of things for zombies, which is "*You die. You kill.*") Importantly, Rick does not say, "*If* you kill, *then* you die." He is not making an if-then proposition (though many have interpreted it this way). Rather, Rick is *accurately describing the situation in which the zombies and humans now find themselves.* For humans to survive in the apocalyptic wasteland, they must become killers—at least of zombies and probably also of other humans. That is, there are no longer any innocents. Nobody who has made it this far has done so without blood on his or her hands.

Zombies, which almost always have blood on their hands (and mouths and necks), are thus unrestrained by the compunction that moved Rick even to articulate his new law. If you kill, you die . . . Right, but you're probably going to die anyway. Also, *everybody is already killing and maiming everybody else, all the time.* (Seriously, have you been paying attention to these comics?) And so Rick heroically shakes the lesser humans from their old ways and pushes them into a new, zombielike way of being with the codification of his important new observation.

You kill. You die. These are the things we are going to be doing from now on. Any questions?

Indeed, it is during this time in the prison that Rick comes closest to understanding that being like the zombies is the only ticket to survival (I don't say salvation) for his flock. He also goes a little overboard in his enthusiasm—which, in retrospect, I think can be forgiven. During a screed on their need to adjust to the new landscape around them, Rick reminds his followers that banks will never be open again, that traditional government will never function as it once did, and that humans must forever change their notions of appropriate interaction with one another.

With you so far, Rick. Right on.

But then he caps it off with "We *are* the walking dead!"

And it's like, um, we need to have a little talk, Rick. I'm going to try to do this as gently as possible, bro.

Remember when you were growing up and there was always that puny neighborhood kid who wanted to tag along with your friends and play games with you, but he totally sucked and you never wanted him around? But your mother would always be like, "Be nice to him and bring him along!" So you would just kind of dutifully obey your mother, even though you didn't really want the kid near you. Remember *that* kid? Good. Now let's say you and your friends are playing baseball, and the puny kid shows up and you let him play, but everybody kind of goes easy on him, you know? The pitches are real fat and over the plate.

Nobody hits a hard grounder right at him. That sort of thing. Okay, so now let's say the game is over and the puny kid just happens to be on the winning team, like randomly. But suddenly, out of nowhere, the kid grows this huge ego and starts taunting the other team and saying, "Oh yeah! I'm a winner! I rule!!!"

Remember how you instantly wanted to smack his puny face and remind him who was boss?

Yeah, so, let's just not get crazy here in this zombie-surrounded prison, Rick. The fact that you're so far along on the road to acting like zombies is great. The fact that you've survived this long—by emulating zombies—is remarkable. You're doing awesome for someone who's just a human. But also, *you're just a human.* You're not an *actual* zombie. Are we 100 percent clear on that? You need to watch how full of yourself you're getting.

After Rick and *some* of his band survive their ordeal in the abandoned prison, they meet a wayward preacher who offers them a place to stay in the form of his abandoned church. However, Rick's new group soon finds themselves being hunted by hostile humans in the area near the church—hunted for food!

When this becomes clear, does Rick smack his forehead and say, "Dude, why didn't *I* think of that? Eating humans, like zombies do—it's so *obvious*!" No, he doesn't. He doesn't because Rick understands that zombies are killers, not cannibals. Zombies don't eat other zombies. Zombies pursue that which is "the other" and still living. The undead do not feed on the undead, and the living would not be emulating zombies by feeding on other living.

Rick rightly apprehends that these misguided human flesh eaters can't hold a candle to actual zombies. And when the cannibals eat from a human who has been bitten by a zombie—resulting in wonderfully chilling cries of "Tainted meat!"—the poverty of this model becomes increasingly clear. Rather than adopting their cannibalistic ways, Rick and his team wisely show contempt for the cannibals (and then brutally kill them). Instead of violating the rule of no zombie-on-zombie violence, Rick drives home that anyone who raises his hand against you becomes "the other" and your enemy. Just as wearing a Superman outfit doesn't let you fly—it's, you know, the superpowers—eating humans doesn't make you as cool and kickass as a zombie, especially if you suck in every other demonstrable way. That's the hard lesson these cannibals have just learned, courtesy of Rick.

When Rick and company reach the outskirts of Washington, D.C., they are met by a group of friendly humans living in a fenced compound. The people in this compound, led by a former U.S. congressman, have created a life for themselves that mimics the old ways before the walking dead. Surrounded by a zombie-proof wall, these humans have cultivated something close to a life of leisure. They throw cocktail parties, take strolls for pleasure, and even work nine-to-five jobs. What payment is demanded in return for this decadent lifestyle? A resident must lose his or her edge—both figuratively and literally.

The residents of this utopia must surrender their awesomely cool guns and swords and other kickass weapons and leave things like "law enforcement" and "zombie killing" up to appointed members of the community. This, of course, is the one thing Rick is *not* willing to do. Rick is the law and order in this new community and realizes it will be incumbent on him to retain the ability to use force. Joined by other members of his band, Rick steals into the community's firearms cache and takes some weapons for himself. This action later proves prudent. *Very* prudent. And this should be obvious, because it is very zombielike.

A zombie never willingly surrenders the things that make it a violent, ass-kicking machine. A zombie cannot be convinced to remove its flesh-rending teeth or its cornea-gouging fingernails. *Nothing* can persuade a zombie to function as anything other than a brain-eating dynamo of maximum possible effectiveness. You can cut off a zombie's fingers, or pull the teeth from its head with a pair of pliers—when we meet Michonne, she is leading two zombies whose jawbones have been removed entirely—but zombies will never willingly participate in such a gelding. Michonne's appearance is so striking because it confirms that she's such a badass. Zombies would never willingly give of their jawbones; thus, we deduce that Michonne has taken them.

When a resident of the new utopia turns out to be a wife beater and child abuser, Rick busts in and sets things right. With his gun. And while the members of this new community are initially loath to condone Rick's actions, the elders see the true quality that this betrays: leadership. Far from making Rick a dangerous rule breaker, his quick-to-violence, zombielike actions have instead proved that he is the smartest, most able person in the entire compound.

Not as cool as an *actual* zombie, but still, you know, pretty good.

Finally, Rick can be vindicated as the actualization of *The Walking Dead*'s ultimate zombie-man by the way his awesomeness is passed on to those around him. Just as zombies transmit a virus with a bite, Rick passes along the traits needed to survive in a zombie apocalypse to those around him by being a model of zombie ass-kickery. When they first meet him, many of Rick's followers are unsure of themselves and ill adapted to surviving in the horrible new reality of the zombie world. Not all of his followers are able to make the switch to being like Rick. (His "conversion rate" is significantly less than that of a real zombie.) But those who *do* mimic Rick and allow themselves to be "infected" by his traits always find themselves the better for it. Andrea goes from victim-in-waiting to sniper queen. Glenn gains confidence and assertiveness, in both his personal life and in his ability to kick ass. Michonne finds a mental toughness and focus that complement her copious skills with a katana blade and render her more effective. Abraham is haunted by the unthinking ease with which he can kill, but Rick helps him find ways to make this trait an asset, not a burden.

But perhaps no transformation is more positive or more touching than the transformation of Rick's own son, Carl. At the end of his encounter with the cannibals, Carl tearfully reveals to Rick, "I killed Ben," referring to a deceased member of the party whose unpredictable nature, and possible mental illness, threatened the safety of the entire group. Though only a boy like Carl, Ben had all the characteristics of a disinterested psychopath when he slaughtered his own brother, Billy. Yet, as Carl reveals, while all of the adults were dithering about what to do, he stepped up and did what needed to be done.

Here, Rick finally has proof that *his own child* has been "infected" by the self-reliant murderousness and mistrust that have allowed Rick himself to survive and triumph for so long.

Rick is silent during Carl's disclosure, and his thoughts are not revealed to us. However, if Rick is feeling anything at this haunting, beautiful moment, it can only be a profound sense of pride in his son's ability to become so perfectly like a zombie.

SCOTT KENEMORE is the author of the undead-themed satires *The Zen of Zombie, Z.E.O., The Art of Zombie Warfare*, and *The Code of the Zombie Pirate*. His first novel, *Zombie, Ohio*, was published in 2011 by Skyhorse Publishing. He is a founding member of the Advisory

Board of the Zombie Research Society, and an active member of the HWA. His short fiction has appeared in *The Kenyon Review*, *Mudrock*, and *Rhonny Reaper's Creature Features Anthology*. He lives in Chicago. Online at scottkenemore.wordpress.com.

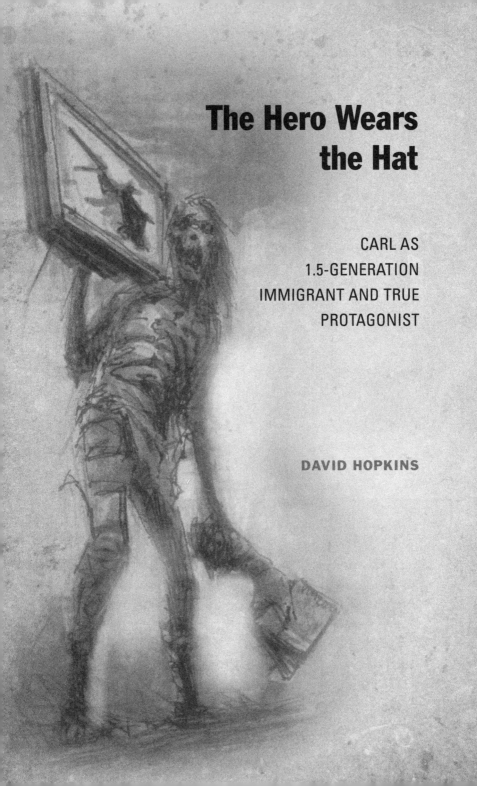

The Hero Wears the Hat

CARL AS 1.5-GENERATION IMMIGRANT AND TRUE PROTAGONIST

DAVID HOPKINS

Two children, a girl and a boy, hold hands. The boy wears a cowboy hat and a bandana tied around his neck. In front of them is a tall chain-link fence. A few yards farther away, there is another fence and then another. Beyond that, clutching, clawing, and snarling, is an uncountable mass of zombies. The children face the zombies, taking it all in. The boy turns to the girl.

"You—are you still *scared* of them?"

"I was. I *used* to be. I still don't like the *sounds* they make, but I'm not *scared* of them anymore. Mostly I just feel sorry for them."

This moment in issue twenty-one of *The Walking Dead* says much about the series and how people acclimate to a new world. As an ongoing comic book, *The Walking Dead* has always been about the long-term effects of a zombie apocalypse—not just how a group of people escape the farmhouse when zombies surround it and not just how a group of people escape the mall when zombies surround it, but how people live day after day, year after year, when zombies occupy and overwhelm their world. The zombie films that involve groups of people escaping from various buildings (yes, I broke the code) are primarily about immediate survival. *The Walking Dead* goes further. This story is not only about survival but also about immigration—people entering into a new habitat and finding their place within it.

The two children, Sophia and Carl, represent the future for humanity in a dangerous world. They stare down that horde on the other side of the fence with the same determination as the huddled masses that crowded the ships sailing to America. While the adults may be the ones who push forward, they do so largely to secure a better life for their children. The children are the ones who will adapt to this new territory in a way the adults never will. When viewed as an immigrant story, *The Walking Dead* has its true protagonist in Carl.

As is the case for any immigrant, the new world poses many dangers. The rules have changed. The territory is more brutal, more unforgiving, and it must be navigated. The characters in *The Walking Dead* must learn the language. I mean language in the broadest sense. More than a communication system, it's a complex code for organizing and making sense of the world. When immigrants "learn the language," they possess the ability to integrate into a culture. The language allows them to survive in hostile territory. In *The Walking Dead*, this means the characters learn how to sleep lightly, travel as a group, and find food and shelter. They learn to assess threats and to be as leery of a new group of people as they are of the zombie fifty yards away. The world never ceases to be dangerous, but as the immigrant adapts, he or she is not caught off guard as often.

This essay covers the *Walking Dead* comics series through issue eighty-four, the last of the "No Way Out" story arc. I note this because of a growing fear that as I type these words, Robert Kirkman could be at his computer writing an elaborate death for Carl—the character I just named as the true protagonist. Not that survival is a prerequisite. Fans of the series know that Kirkman can kill any character in *The Walking Dead* at any moment. Currently, of the 107 comic book characters listed in the *Walking Dead* wiki, 75 are already dead. As soon as a character becomes too precious or too popular, some roamer approaches from behind, tears him or her to shreds, and the reader is left holding the book, wondering what the hell happened. Fans of the series remember the tragic, unexpected deaths of Amy, Tyreese, Hershel, Lori, Judith, and Dale. No one is safe. Most people consider Rick Grimes the main character. He has been with us since page one of the first issue, yet no one would be surprised if Rick died. In an interview with Newsarama on January 14, 2009, Kirkman said, "If I keep doing horrible things to that guy [Rick Grimes], I'm going to eventually *have* to kill him or this book will become completely unrealistic."

Viewing Carl as the protagonist does not come from wishful thinking that he can outlast everyone else. Instead, through observing what he has learned and how he has changed, we see that Carl represents a larger story about the first generation to come of age at the end of the world. Whether Carl is living, dead, or undead, his journey embodies the immigration themes so essential to this series.

LANGUAGE OF A NEW WORLD

Carl Grimes is a member of the 1.5 generation in zombieland. The term "1.5 generation," coined by Ruben Rumbaut of the University of California–Irvine, refers to people who immigrate with their parents to a new country during their childhood. "Those who came between ages six and twelve are the classic 1.5ers," Rumbaut told Leslie Berestein Rojas for an article on the website Multi-American. "They are truly in-between." They assimilate more easily into the culture than adults. However, unlike the second generation born into the new country, the 1.5 generation retains aspects of both the old and new cultures. They are the bilingual children who act as interpreters for their parents, who might not have been able to make the adjustment as easily.

In *The Walking Dead*, the new language is, in part, adjusting to a new morality. This new morality is as much a survival skill as learning to be cautious of any odd noises that might signal the presence of zombies. The old-world morality relied on due process, the hope of rehabilitation, and the possibility of clemency as a way to maintain order. In the new world, trust is never fully given, and judgment is highly subjective. Due process is a waste of time. Rehabilitation is a waste of resources, and clemency might get you killed.

In the "Safety Behind Bars" story arc, the prisoner Thomas claims he was incarcerated for tax evasion. He seems friendly and harmless enough. Then he decapitates Susie and Rachel. He attacks Andrea with a knife, and Andrea escapes with her cheek torn from ear to mouth. When Rick sees Thomas chasing Andrea with a knife, he punches Thomas' face to pulp. Rick offers cruel justice: hang the bastard. A sympathetic Patricia tries to help Thomas escape. Thomas starts to strangle her, and Maggie shoots Thomas in the back several times. No one complains. Patricia's old-world morality (clemency) clearly did not work. There was some early resistance to Rick's methods in the series. However, he did not leave much room for discussion. "An eye for an eye, a tooth for a tooth" is cruel but efficient. The adults learn this horrible truth one retribution killing after another: Tyreese chokes Chris to death, Rick shoots Dexter in the head, Michonne cuts off various limbs from the Governor, Andrea shoots Gabe in the head, Rick cuts the roadside bandit to pieces, the group tortures and kills the suburban cannibals, and Rick shoots Pete in the head.

Carl and the other children witness many of these events, taking it all in. They remember the old world, at least vaguely, but they more quickly accept this cruel judgment. At first, Carl worries his dad has gone crazy. He says to his mother, "He just *attacked* that man. He wouldn't stop *hitting* him, Mom. Why did he hit him so *much*?" Once Carl's mother explains that he was a bad man, this resolves any confusion. Carl understands these measures, possibly remembering when he killed Shane in issue six. Shane had his rifle aimed at Rick, ready to fire, and Carl shot him in the throat. He's a bad guy; he must be killed.

I LEARNED IT BY WATCHING YOU

Father/son themes abound in the series, because the story of a 1.5-generation immigrant begins with the first-generation immigrants: the parents who bring their children to this new world, who work to give them a better life. After Rick wakes from his coma, the first living people he meets are a father and son, Morgan and Duane. Rick takes the father and son to the police station's armory. Morgan tells Duane he'll teach him to fire a gun tomorrow: a father takes his first steps to empower his son in a dangerous world. In issue fifty-eight, Morgan returns to the series. Duane is now a zombie. Even when a father tries to prepare his son for the new world, he can't always protect him. In a sense, Duane merges into the dominant culture, which drives Morgan insane. Rick convinces Abraham that Morgan should join the group, saying, "He's no different than we are, Abraham. We do terrible things for the ones we love."

At the beginning of the series, soon after Rick reunites with his family at the Atlanta campsite, he leaves again to find more guns. "This has to be done so we can all be *safe*," he says. He promises to teach Carl how to shoot when he returns. His wife, Lori, still holding to old-world attitudes, says seven-year-olds are too young to have a gun. Later, after Susie and Rachel are murdered, Lori reconsiders her feelings: "*Christ*. I was going to take Carl's gun away *today*. I thought we were *safe*. Maybe if Rachel and Susie had guns . . ." In the old world, a young child with a gun would be absurd. In the new world, while guns often pose as many problems as they solve, leaving your child defenseless is unconscionable.

When Rick offers Carl a gun, he also gives him his hat. The gun and the hat are potent mythic symbols in *The Walking Dead*. Consider that the hero in Joseph Campbell's monomyth is essentially an immigrant, moving from the familiar world into the unknown. The receiving of gifts is an important component. Like in the Arthurian legends surrounding Excalibur and the Holy Grail, the hero may be unlikely yet willing to take the call in order to receive these items. One is an item of power and authority. The other is an item of responsibility and calling. For Carl, the gun is power, but to wear a lawman's hat—a cowboy hat—means Carl must be a vigilante and pure in his use of power. An officer of the law must serve and protect his community; the gun is "protect," and the hat is "serve." They are symbols of heroic, rugged masculinity, and Rick offers them to his son and teaches him to use the power and responsibility appropriately. Is Rick anointing, or deputizing, his successor in the *Walking Dead* epic? Like so many immigrants, the son is expected not only to replace the father but to move into new territory with the father's wisdom.

The gun and the hat are very dear to Carl. You rarely see him without them. Carl holds the hat when he sleeps. In part, it's an emotional attachment, but it *is* a lawman's hat, and the deep meaning it carries is not lost on Carl. In issue ten, after he wakes from the surgery to remove the bullet from his shoulder, the first words out of his mouth are "Where's my *hat*? [. . .] Nobody *better* not've taken my *hat*!"

Soon after receiving his gun, Carl uses it to protect his mother when zombies raid the campsite, and later he pulls it to save his father. When Hershel puts a gun to Rick's head, asking them to leave, Carl draws his gun, ready and determined. And yet, the gun is an old-world weapon with serious flaws. Every time a gun is fired, there's a possibility it will attract the attention of hundreds of zombies. Rick constantly warns his group to not use their guns. Michonne has been far more effective with her samurai sword. In issue fifty-seven, Carl dreamily watches Michonne kill zombies with her sword. His only response? "Cool." Why the entire group hasn't raided the Medieval Times in Atlanta for a cache of broadswords is beyond me. The 1.5 generation identifies the value of a sword when most of the adults are still attached to their guns and little else. If Carl is to reach adulthood in the new world, he should have his own sword. And, hey, who wouldn't want to see a samurai cowboy fighting zombies?

LOSING HIS MOTHER, TAKING CARE OF HIS FATHER

As the 1.5-generation immigrant adapts to the new world, a moment comes when he leaves his mother and no longer needs his father's guidance. While this is true for any child, the 1.5 generation adapts so thoroughly that it's a more complete abandonment and takes heroic proportions. At the end of issue forty-eight,

Carl's half-sister, Judith, and his mother, Lori, are killed during the Woodbury invasion. Carl and Rick escape by running the gauntlet of zombies that surround the prison. This gauntlet is the true beginning of Carl's passage into adulthood. It leads to his trial in the wilderness. When Campbell's mythic hero enters into the unknown, he must face trials that carry special significance— as any immigrant will face trials that test him in the new world.

In the next issue, only father and son remain. They have been separated from the rest of the group, and they're in bad shape. Rick, now with only one hand, needs help with basic tasks such as opening a can for food. Carl, depressed, will not eat. Once they arrive in an abandoned town, it is clear Rick cannot take care of himself. He is weak from a gunshot to his stomach. A zombie surprises them. Rick chops at its head, but the axe doesn't go deep enough to destroy it. Carl shoots the zombie to save his dad, and they take refuge in a house. Rick is sick from the infected gunshot wound, and he collapses, unconscious. Carl thinks his father is dead and may rise again as undead. This is Carl's first wilderness test. He aims the gun at his father. Can he kill his father if he turns into a zombie? This moment illustrates the impossible ethical situations of a cruel world. The young son, his back against the wall in a dark room, breathes deeply; his gun is drawn and aimed at his father lying on the ground. Carl ultimately doesn't shoot his dad, but he was ready.

In Carl's second test, he confronts the zombies, and he survives. He lures two of the walking dead from the house. When surprised by a third, he kills them all at point-blank range. Carl returns to the house and yells at his unconscious father, angry with him for his inability to protect the people in their group:

You can't protect anyone! But me—I can protect myself. Probably better than any of those people . . . better than you could.

You still think I'm a kid—but I'm not. I don't want to play with toys anymore. I don't get scared like I used to. I'm not a kid anymore.

Here we get a glimpse of Carl Grimes as the hero, the samurai cowboy of the apocalypse. The moment of bravado fades when Carl believes once again that his father has died. The first test returns, but he can't do it. "I can't be *alone*. I'm just a kid—I can't live on my own . . . ," he says. Fortunately, Rick returns to health, and they resume their journey. A third test will come later.

KILLING BEN

The 1.5 generation of *The Walking Dead* surprises their first-generation parents with how coldly they respond to death. In issue three, Sophia wonders if her dad will come back, and Carl, without pity, reminds Sophia that her dad is dead. This scene is only the first example of Carl's harshness. In issue forty-seven, Rick tells Carl that Tyreese has died and asks him if he is upset. Carl's response scares Rick: "No, people die, Dad. It happens all the time. I'll miss Tyreese . . . but I knew he was going to die eventually. Everyone will. Everyone." Then, in issue seventy-seven, when Carl walks in on Rick pretending to talk with Lori on his phone, Carl's reaction is hardly sympathetic: "This is *weird*, Dad. Mom is *dead*. You *can't* talk to her. You sure as hell can't talk to her on a *stupid phone*." With death all around, Carl has grown numb. It's an understandable coping mechanism.

Is this new world turning all the children into emotionless sociopaths? In issue sixty, Ben mutilates a cat and asks his twin brother Billy not to tell anyone. In the next issue, he murders

Billy—gutting him with a knife, unaware he has done anything wrong. Is this the new morality? It's the darker side of coping, but there's also the option of the hero immigrant. A sociopath has complete disregard for others, but Carl makes the decision to kill Ben with full knowledge of the consequences. He knows Ben is dangerous and needs to be eliminated, just as the group has exterminated dangerous adults, such as Thomas, in the past. Carl also knows the adults won't be able to do it. This is Carl's third test in the new world. He has to kill his friend. As Carl later confesses to his father, it was not easy. This test shows that Carl can make the tough choices. An immigrant sacrifices much in his journey. Innocence is often the first possession left on the far shore.

When Carl sneaks off to kill Ben, he leaves his hat behind, which is significant. Sure, he does it in part to make Rick think he is still in the tent, sleeping soundly. But since the hat represents the ethical use of power, by leaving it behind, Carl acknowledges he's operating outside the old law. Like his father, he does what needs to be done. Ben asks innocently, "Are you scared of me?" Carl's face is the darkest it has ever been, almost entirely in shadow. He says no and pulls the trigger.

This is not the first time Carl has taken a life, but killing Ben is different from killing Shane. The first killing was a gut reaction. In the case of Ben, Carl has to make a choice, one that takes planning. Shane knew what he was doing, but Ben is mentally ill and unaware he has done anything wrong. In the old world, as Abraham Ford points out, Ben would get "twenty years of therapy" and they'd still never fix him. In the new world, there's only one fix. Zombies are a predictable and constant danger, but the living are still the most wildly erratic menace in *The Walking Dead*. Carl's decision is a difficult one and proves that he has learned the language of a hostile new world.

IT SHOULD NEVER BE EASY

It takes a tough person to survive as an immigrant. *The Walking Dead* suggests that the old world was soft. Turn to the back of any of the trade paperback collections. The text is the same with each volume:

> How many hours are in a day when you don't spend half of them watching television? When is the last time any of us really worked to get something that we wanted? The world we knew is gone. The world of commerce and frivolous necessity has been replaced by a world of survival and responsibility. In a world ruled by the dead, we are forced to finally start living.

Life was too easy. The zombies are the antagonists, but they are also the victims—the ones who weren't strong enough to survive. Those remaining must get tougher. Some of the first-generation immigrants are ahead of the curve. Rick, Michonne, Andrea, Abraham, and Tyreese adapt well. They protect the weaker members of the group and distribute justice when necessary, an important component of the new morality. It's the 1.5 generation that will truly learn how to care for themselves.

After Carl kills Shane, he starts crying, hugs his dad, and says, "It's not the same as killing the *dead* ones, Daddy." To which Rick responds, "It never *should* be." This bit of comfort echoes the advice he gives to Carl in issue sixty-seven after Carl confesses to killing Ben: "When we do these things and we're good people . . . they're still *bad* things. You can never lose sight of that. If these things start becoming *easy*, that's when it's all over. That's when we become bad people." It should never be easy to make the hard decisions. If so, we become psychopaths like the Governor or the suburban cannibals, unfeeling in our murderous nature. It's hard to judge if this advice is for Carl or if this is a word of caution to Rick himself. Rick has lost it at times. He has gone too far, and his sense of responsibility to his son seems to be the only thing that keeps him in check. The advice is solid. The old world wanted to make things as easy as possible, but that's a danger in itself. There is a value to struggle. Carl has not shrugged off Ben's death. It does affect him, and he confesses to crying every night. This vulnerability strengthens Carl as the hero who survived the trial in the wilderness. The anguish Carl feels allows him to hold on to his humanity.

In hopes of an easier and better life, the immigrant longs for the proverbial "streets lined with gold," which is ultimately a trap. In *The Walking Dead*, the Alexandria Safe-Zone is this false utopia. Carl knows life will never be easy, and the safe-zone makes him fearful. He isn't able to fully let down his guard. That the children celebrate Halloween deeply disturbs Carl, and he doesn't understand why everyone is pretending the zombies don't exist. Rick encourages him to play, but Carl says, "I don't want to get used to this—it'll make us *weak*. I don't want to die." Carl believes that if they let down their guard, they will become soft and vulnerable by the time they must leave. Rick takes Carl back to their house.

It's true. Carl understands nothing good can last for very long, and this is even more true in the new world. No walls are strong enough. If the prison can fall, then the Alexandria Safe-Zone can fall too. The immigrants who pretend they can recreate the old world deceive themselves. Indeed, in the "No Way Out" story arc, the wall in the Alexandria Safe-Zone is breached, and zombies storm the community. As the group fights back, a stray bullet strikes Carl in the face. Rick takes Carl to Dr. Cloyd, demanding that she save him. As Rick and Michonne fight the horde of zombies, the others are emboldened to join in the fight, and they overcome amazing odds. Afterward, Rick sits at Carl's bedside and ponders what transpired: "I think about the road ahead of us, and for the first time it seems long . . . and bright. After everything we've been through, all the people we've lost . . . I suddenly find myself overcome with something I thought we'd lost . . . *hope*." Rick clearly sees the future as a place that will be inviting to the next generation. "I want to show you this new world. I want to make it a reality for you. Please, Carl—live so that I can show you."

A GLIMPSE OF THE FUTURE

Robert Kirkman says in the introduction to the first volume that he envisioned *The Walking Dead* as "the zombie movie that never ends." Then he notes, "I hope you guys are looking forward to a sprawling epic, because that's the idea with this one." How sprawling and epic the sprawling epic will be remains to be seen. Carl's hat doesn't fit right now, but it fits better now than it did when he first started his journey through the new world. His is the immigrant's story about finding the right fit, growing into the role that has been thrust upon him. Carl stands on one side of the fence waiting to be cast into the new world, to make his own path—wherever that may lead.

DAVID HOPKINS is a comic book writer and essayist, a contributor to *D Magazine* and *Quick*. In addition to this essay, he's written for Smart Pop's *Man from Krypton* and *Webslinger*. For the past eleven years, he's taught English and creative writing at Martin High School. David lives in Arlington, Texas, with daughter Kennedy and his fiancée April. David once sat across from Robert Kirkman during a comic book convention brunch. It was cool. Online at antiherocomics.com or follow David on Twitter @davidhopkins.

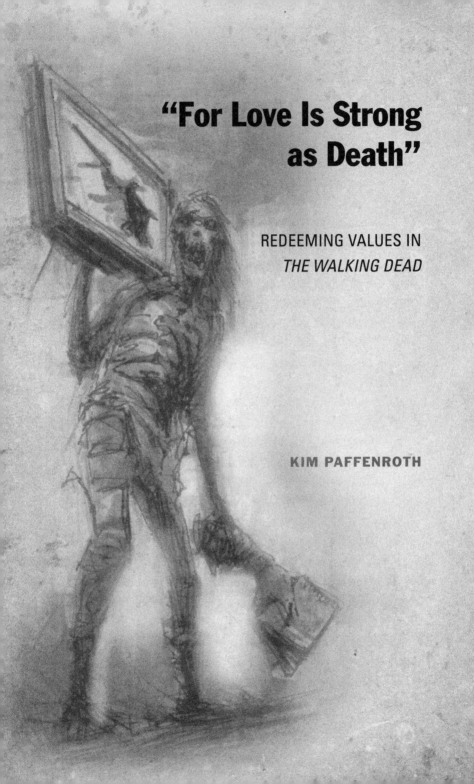

"For Love Is Strong as Death"

REDEEMING VALUES IN *THE WALKING DEAD*

KIM PAFFENROTH

One of my best friends recently admitted he could not get into *The Walking Dead*, or zombie literature or films in general, because they are too hopeless, their characters' actions too futile. Nothing matters in the world of zombies, and the constant work of killing and fleeing is never-ending and pointless. One can behave bravely or stoically, but to what purpose? Anyone temporarily "saved" from a dire fate is usually only killed in some equally horrible way later on. This is a fairly common—and straightforward and understandable—criticism of the zombie subgenre. However, it is one that applies least to *The Walking Dead*.

To show how different this new series is from its predecessors and contemporaries, let's first examine George Romero's *Night of the Living Dead* (1968), because it is the seminal zombie film that every new artist knows and references—whether directly or indirectly—and thus stands as the paradigmatic zombie narrative: people are trapped somewhere with a growing zombie horde outside, and we watch the cohesion of their group unravel to the point at which the zombies can get the upper hand. The bare bones of the plot of *Night of the Living Dead* show how close it is to the setup of *The Walking Dead*: although the human survivors are more mobile in the latter, the focus on interpersonal dynamics and conflicts remains the central point of the series. But in tone and resolution, the first of the modern zombie films and the recent television series differ. *Night of the Living*

Dead is a story of unrelenting despair, filling us by the end with only dread and hopelessness—what critic Richard McGuinness of *The Village Voice* aptly called a "gluey, bottomless horror." *The Walking Dead* is hardly upbeat or optimistic, and the series continues much of Romero's pessimism about human potential and the general sense of nihilism found in most zombie films and literature. But in some small but important ways, *The Walking Dead* finds a greater sense of redemption—or at least the possibility of redemption—than does Romero's dark vision of *Night of the Living Dead*, which most other directors and writers have perpetuated and expanded.

Romero's classic taunts us with many graphic horrors: disfigured corpses walking around, zombies feasting on bloody body parts, two of the least unlikable characters being burned alive, and another losing her sanity at the threat of becoming one of "them." The casual or first-time viewer is probably most captivated, and disgusted, by this aspect of Romero's art. But a closer examination of the film reveals that Romero's shock and disgust go deeper than the surface spectacle; the movie is a critique of society and even human nature, at which viewers become equally shocked and disgusted. As the people huddle in the farmhouse, surrounded by the living dead, they consume a constant stream of misinformation from the television. Even the discovery of the television is presented with dark humor: the character Helen is lured out of the relative safety of the basement when she's told there is a working television upstairs, but the discovery soon proves empty, a false promise of information. The more they pay attention to the television and try to follow its commands, the more they worsen their predicament. The advice it gives is conflicted—first telling them to stay in the house, when they might have been able to get out before more zombies assembled outside, and then telling them to get to a rescue station, when trying to refuel the truck and drive to the station at the height of the attack leads to members of the group being killed and eaten. Though many would argue that, at the time, television images were a positive source of information that helped, for example, fuel opposition to the war in Vietnam, Romero seems here to register serious misgivings about the medium. For him, television leads to a naïve addiction and a trust that distracts us from seeing how things really are and paying attention to the problems right in front of us.

Romero continues this critique of the media in his later films. *Dawn of the Dead* (1978) begins with a news broadcast that knowingly sends people to overrun rescue stations where they will surely be eaten. *Land of the Dead* (2005) features a post-apocalyptic society that relies on misleading television commercials to keep its perpetual underclass ignorant and satisfied. And *Diary of the Dead* (2007) is a parody of our culture's attempt—through the internet and cell phones—to see news as it happens; a recurring clip in the film shows a zombie attack in the initial hours of the outbreak, but the film is later shown to have been doctored so that people do not realize the severity of what's happening until it's too late.

The television reports that the characters in *Night of the Living Dead* watch include interviews with government officials, so these officials are implicated in the general failure to help the protagonists survive the undead onslaught. The problem of the dead rising is vaguely attributed to some kind of "radiation" from a returning space probe, so science is also to blame; it's the cause of human destruction, not its cure or salvation. The military and law enforcement are mostly absent in this installment of Romero's zombie saga, but he has left plenty of evidence that he would see them as destructive forces that may be good at killing zombies but might ultimately destroy any sense of humaneness, decency, or value among the living. At the end of *Night of the Living Dead*, the posse led by the "sheriff" is brutal and careless in its killing, wiping out the last of the protagonists who had survived the attack of the undead. Similarly out-of-control bands of roving killers are seen at the beginning of the sequel, *Dawn of the Dead* (1978); and *Day of the Dead* (1985), *Diary of the Dead* (2007), and *Survival of the Dead* (2009) all feature military units that are basically armed bands of thugs preying on other survivors. Romero only hints at the inefficacy of religion, but there is no reason to think it would offer any more aid or comfort than the other failed human institutions of the military, government, media, or scientific communities. In fact, as Gregory A. Waller remarks in *The Living and the Undead: From Stoker's "Dracula" to Romero's "Dawn of the Dead,"* the character who repeatedly falls back on her faith, Barbra, is not helped by it one bit: "Traditional rituals offer her no protection, her veneration of the dead is pointless, and it makes no difference whether she demonstrates Christian faith."

The Walking Dead follows up on many of these typical post-apocalyptic themes: the major institutions that order human life—the media, the government, the military, science, and religion—are as ineffective in the new series as they were in 1968, though *The Walking Dead* often devotes differing amounts of attention to each one. By the time the story begins, the media is already gone, so there is less indictment of it. However, as Rick hears the details of what has happened, it is revealed that people have been told by the government and media to go to Atlanta, which has resulted in many more dying, and subsequently becoming undead, than if they had stayed away. There are police and military vehicles scattered all over a ruined Atlanta, so clearly these were ineffectual in the battles that occurred there. Worse, in one flashback to the initial outbreak, military personnel are shown slaughtering the doctors, nurses, and patients at the hospital where Rick lay in a coma. However, on the issue of authority figures and their relative good or evil, *The Walking Dead* registers more optimism than Romero's work: Rick's continued wearing of his police uniform is a constant reminder that a more hopeful outcome is possible—that Rick will help establish new, more honest and effective forms of law and order in the fledgling community than prevailed in a pre-zombie United States.

With the group's journey to seek help at the Centers for Disease Control (CDC) building, the show offers a much more explicit critique of science than does Romero's work. (It is also a major difference between the television series and the comics, which lack the CDC plotline.) In *The Walking Dead*, the CDC appears as something of a gigantic monument to the failure of technology. Its high-tech fortress in the midst of a wasteland can provide comfort, even pampering, with hot water and fine wine, but those who built its technological wonders were unable to stop the epidemic, to cure the ensuing madness and hopelessness of the survivors, or to assuage the guilt or grief of the living. By the time the protagonists of the *Walking Dead* television series show up, it is clear that the psychological damage caused by widespread suffering and death is the more fundamental problem and the one technology is least equipped to address or even acknowledge. The center is deserted, abandoned by everyone except Dr. Jenner, driven mad by his helplessness and grief. He stays on simply because he has no better place to wait to die, and his despair nearly drags all the survivors into his suicide plan. The technological wonders and temporary comforts do nothing to stop our slightly tipsy survivors from escalating the violence and recriminations they hurl at one another. In one of the tensest moments of the series, the whole group is almost wiped out by the building's defenses and its HAL-like computer.

Although Romero suggests at least vaguely a possibly scientific source of the zombie outbreak, the "mysterious radiation" from a satellite, *The Walking Dead* does not offer an explanation. Significantly, the show does not follow many other recent zombie works (e.g., *28 Days Later* and the *Resident Evil* franchise) in explicitly blaming the catastrophe on scientists and their deliberate or accidental creation of the outbreak. Instead, it critiques the materialistic assumptions of modern science, as epitomized by the awesome technology of the CDC: science is not blamed for the plague, but it is shown to offer the survivors nothing that can cure their psychological pain or moral failings—the cure they really need to survive. In the end, all the CDC facility can do is try to incinerate them like another infection intruding on its orderly and inhuman existence. Given Rick's insistence that they run serious risks to seek out the help of the CDC in the first place, this is a huge turning point: whatever goodness or hope they find in their journey will not come from a reestablishment of technological dominance over the natural world.

If Rick and the others hope to find something better than technology by reaffirming or rediscovering religion, they would seem to be in for as much disappointment as any of Romero's characters. The references to religion in the first season of *The Walking Dead* are muted and scattered, especially in comparison to the comics, which have the explicitly religious characters of Hershel Greene and Father Stokes. So far in the television series, the most religious scene comes when Morgan's son, Duane, insists they say grace over their meal. The scene is touching but implies that religiosity is childish and naïve, because it does nothing to improve their situation or equip them to deal with their harsh reality. Likewise, it is unclear how the father and son will ultimately deal with Duane's now-zombified mother. In the "regular" world, religion provides ceremonies to mark the transition from life to death and rituals to help the survivors cope with grief, but those are useless in the family's new situation. Cold rationality would dictate she be terminated for safety's sake, but Morgan is also unable to do that, though it is unclear whether his hand is stayed by compassion for some residual humanity in her—and therefore, perhaps, a source of strength and hope in his life—or mere sentimentality, which is a paralyzing weakness and not a spiritual strength.

However, the undeniably moving scenes of this family's love continuing in a painful, tragic, zombified world are drastically different from how romantic and familial love are depicted in *Night of the Living Dead*. The loving relationships we form with other people, including romantic attachments and ties between parents, children, and siblings, are, for most of us, the most fundamental and constant source of meaning and purpose in our lives. It is the undermining of these relationships and the trust we put in them that makes *Night of the Living Dead* truly unsettling. With the scene in the basement, in which the undead child, Karen, first gnaws on her dead father's arm and then stabs her mother fourteen times with a trowel, we see how far Romero's nihilism extends—not just to rejecting human institutions but even to showing a perverted, fatal side to the deepest human relationships. As Robin Wood notes in his essay, "Apocalypse Now: Notes on the Living Dead," in *American Nightmare: Essays on the Horror Film*, "Their destruction at the hands of their zombie daughter represents the film's judgment on them and the norm they embody."

And what is played out with the darkest horror for Karen and her parents is played out with slightly more comic overtones for Barbra and her brother (and their apparently dysfunctional relationship with their parents), and in the more pathetic, ironic behaviors of the young couple, Judy and Tom. Relationships, it seems, are a part of what traps and kills us, and zombies just accelerate and make explicit a process that was already ongoing in the lives of the protagonists before, whether they bickered and blamed one another or cloyingly and codependently clung to one another.

In one way, *The Walking Dead* falls right in line with Romero's work. When a character's familial love becomes too narrow and obsessive, he or she cannot survive the loss of that relationship, as we see with Dr. Jenner and Jim. But otherwise, the contrast between *The Walking Dead* and Romero's more pessimistic view could not be more remarkable and pronounced. Love for his wife and child is what keeps Rick going as he fights his way across a zombie-infested Georgia. Morgan is strongly driven by both love and grief, as he fights to keep his son alive and to give him some sense of sanity and stability, even as he struggles with himself to end his wife's undead existence. The sisters Andrea and Amy seem to have a relationship that, at least momentarily, deepens and becomes more intimate and loving in the horrible zombie world—a bond that had perhaps withered or loosened in a world with more mundane concerns. Similarly, the widower Dale grows close to the two sisters, loving for the first time since his wife's death, years before. The otherwise unlikable Dixon brothers, Merle and Daryl—generally shown as selfish, brutal, racist, and uncouth—are given their only redeeming characteristic in the fierce loyalty of Daryl to his brother. The appearance of one man's grandmother reveals that the seemingly threatening young Latino men in the barricaded building in Atlanta are, in fact, kind and compassionate protectors of a center full of defenseless seniors.

Love and family are therefore more positive and powerful in *The Walking Dead* than they are in *Night of the Living Dead* or many other current versions of the zombie apocalypse. But are they finally more efficacious, or are the characters powerfully driven only to perform futile actions that can have no ultimate significance? Though it remains to be seen how closely the television series will follow the comics into darker, more violent plot arcs in which love fails because of betrayal or mistrust, so far, love and family are reliable sources of purpose for the characters and are shown to be capable of withstanding the destructive forces of an undead world.

First, the love that family members have for one another several times expands to include others—either reaching outside the original family unit or making the newcomer a part of the family. Morgan and his son do not just defend one another; they extend their decency and compassion to Rick when they discover him, saving him from zombies and enabling him to reunite with his own family. As noted, Dale forms new bonds with Andrea and Amy, despite having given up on personal attachments in the pre-zombie world. (The comics later develop this bond into a romantic, sexual relationship between Dale and Andrea.) Thus, the new zombie world is even helpful to his emotional health, which had sickened under the weight of "regular" grief in the pre-zombie world. The young men protecting the seniors in Atlanta adopt others and widen their "family" to include not just those related by blood; they also show themselves to be fair and generous to Rick and his group, who reciprocate the kindness. The ethnic and racial suspicion and violence that had thrived in the "real" world (and still have their proponents, as with the Dixon brothers) are shown being dismantled in the "uncivilized," postapocalyptic Georgia. In a world where the dead walk, the living find it all the more imperative—and sometimes, ironically, even easier—to love one another.

Love is also shown to be stronger than (un)death in the series when we consider what the most urgent threats to our protagonists are. In all Romero's zombie films, the real threat is from other survivors: their various treacheries, greed, selfishness, and cowardice are what eventually kills all the living—through direct violence and by weakening the survivors' defenses to the point where the undead can effectively attack. This concept of the living being more dangerous than the undead is repeated in *The Walking Dead*: most of the time, the survivors are able to move about the streets freely, with the undead scattered, slow, and not much of a threat. Living people, such as Dr. Jenner, have come much closer to wiping out all the protagonists than the zombie hordes have been able to. The undead are a background danger, while the tensions and dramas among the living are in the foreground.

The most serious threat in *The Walking Dead* is from those men who threaten the established family units. To put it bluntly, Shane is the main problem, not the zombies, because he undermines the stability of Rick and Lori's family, which is their motivation to continue living and fighting against the undead. On a practical level, his jealousy and competition threaten the safety of the whole community, because he cannot be relied on to protect others if he envies what they have. Though it is eventually revealed that Shane's actions in the hospital were not as blameworthy as Lori had suspected, he exacerbates the problems and the threat to the group by trying to usurp Rick's role as father and husband, by cozying up to Carl and by having impregnated Lori, and as leader of the group, even to the point of contemplating killing Rick in the penultimate episode of season one.

The most intense violence among the survivors is caused by another man who threatens family stability: the wife beater and general misogynist, Ed. His assault on his wife, Carol, and the other women results in a much bloodier confrontation than even the loss of Merle, the insanity of Jim, or the constant race-baiting of the Dixons—all of which are handled with considerably more restraint than we might have expected in a group of constantly armed people. Once Ed is dead, Carol savages his body with a pickax in a scene quite reminiscent of Karen's desecration of her parents in *Night of the Living Dead*—brains and blood spattering as Carol uses a metal implement to vent her rage against the one who violated and betrayed her love and trust. This new, postapocalyptic community, which relies on family as its only source of purpose, can tolerate bigots and other undesirables—in the name of both unity and safety for the group—but it cannot overlook intrafamily violence or unattached males who threaten to disrupt an already established family unit. As suggested previously, familial love can expand to create communities or even to connect groups of survivors, but within those communities, threats to the family must be opposed with much more violent force than other infractions.

Finally, the love and commitment among the survivors in *The Walking Dead* is sometimes shown to expand to include mercy and compassion even for the living dead. There are hints of this in Romero's work as well, at least after *Night of the Living Dead*, from the pity Fran shows to the nun and Little League zombies in *Dawn of the Dead*, to the glimpses of some residual humanity in Bub in *Day of the Dead* (1985), to the final truce between zombies and humans at the end of *Land of the Dead* (2005). But in *The Walking Dead*, it is a humane gesture seen in most of the episodes. Morgan cannot bring himself to shoot his undead wife. Andrea does shoot her undead sister, but it is one of the most poignant moments in the whole series. It is shockingly juxtaposed with Carol reducing her dead husband's head to pulp, and it contrasts sharply with similar mercy killings in other zombie films, in which the killer usually looks furtive and even embarrassed at what has to be done. For Andrea, it is a last act of love and care. Similarly compassionate, but for a total stranger, is Rick's gesture in the first episode, when he goes out of his way to end the suffering of one horribly disfigured zombie woman, who has been reduced to a torso, clawing her way along the ground. In the next episode, when the survivors have to dismember a zombie's body to use its fluids to camouflage their own scent, Rick takes a moment to learn the dead man's name and his history. In the penultimate episode, Glenn insists that they bury the dead from their own group and not merely burn them. All of these are incidents of sanctification: a world overrun by zombies may be almost unbearably violent and sad, but it need not be unholy and meaningless. The living can choose to honor the dead and respect whatever remains of their humanity, just as they can choose to love one another and find purpose in that love.

In *Night of the Living Dead*, family members are just another thing that kills you, and their special connection to you only makes the killing more horrible, monstrous, and depressing. So far, *The Walking Dead* has presented us with a view of life in which the committed love among family members is the only reliable, if fragile, source of meaning or purpose in an otherwise bleak human existence. In short, the series is as optimistic as a zombie story can be, without completely jumping the shark and having a happy ending in which the living defeat the undead hordes. (This is my one misgiving about Max Brooks' *World War Z*: for all its dark humor and tremendous battle scenes, its ending seems almost to violate the subgenre by having the humans win—and apparently not learn much from their experience, other than that they should now live in houses on stilts). This slight but significant source of hopefulness is more prevalent in the *Walking Dead* television series than it is in the comics, and it is probably a big part of the show's success. The series tempers this optimism with a grim view of American society that is quite close to Romero's own cynicism, but it does not follow Romero's early work in condemning human nature as intrinsically so sick and corrupt that it must self-destruct. In *The Walking Dead*, there are moments of mercy and compassion that are as real as any to be found in a zombie-free world: they are often fleeting, but they are not futile. The bonds of love built and maintained between the main characters could perhaps save them. This precarious, thrilling balance of hope and fear surely helped attract audiences of the show's first season, filling them with a desire to see these people succeed and dread of their potential failures—all of it piqued by the guilty pleasure of seeing the spectacular gore of zombie attacks.

KIM PAFFENROTH is a professor of religious studies at Iona College. He has written several books on theology and the Bible, and, since 2006, has turned his analysis more toward the zombie genre. His examination of Romero's zombie films, *Gospel of the Living Dead: George Romero's Visions of Hell on Earth* (Baylor, 2006), won the Bram Stoker Award. He has also written several zombie novels, including *Dying to Live* and *Valley of the Dead*. Online at gotld.blogspot.com.

{ ACKNOWLEDGMENTS }

Putting together an anthology, like surviving the zombie apocalypse, is an intensely collaborative process, and *Triumph of The Walking Dead* even more so than most. Thanks are due to Glenn Yeffeth, publisher and CEO of BenBella Books, for giving the project such a great home; Heather Butterfield and Jennifer Canzoneri for terrific production and marketing support, respectively; the crack team of copyeditors and designers who made all of us look better; and most especially Leah Wilson, editor-in-chief of the Smart Pop line, for her insightful critiques and unflagging enthusiasm. Outside the scattered and various workspaces that make up BenBella, the book benefited from support and small acts of kindness or professional courtesy from John Joseph Adams, Brendan Deneen, Del Howison, and Tim Seeley.

The anthology would be only so many blank pages without the contributions of the talented essayists, who graciously addressed all editorial queries with good humor and impressive talent. Thanks, too, to their agents, for helping to make their participation possible. Special thanks to legendary storyteller Joe R. Lansdale for gracing us with his foreword (you cannot call yourself a true zombiephile if you have not read his brilliant

"On the Far Side of the Cadillac Desert with Dead Folks"), and to artist Rafael Kayanan, who absolutely nailed the look we were after with his cover illustration.

All of us hope that this essay collection reflects our admiration for *The Walking Dead* and everyone involved in its creation, whether as comic book, prose, or TV series. George A. Romero may have made zombies into the brain-munching menace we know today, but you brought them shuffling into the mainstream in a form worthy of serious commentary—and respect.

JAMES LOWDER has edited book lines or series for both large and small houses, and has helmed such critically acclaimed anthologies as *Curse of the Full Moon* and the Books of Flesh zombie fiction trilogy. As an author, his publications include the bestselling, widely translated dark fantasy novels *Prince of Lies* and *Knight of the Black Rose*, short fiction for such anthologies as *Shadows Over Baker Street*, and comic book scripts for DC, Image, and Moonstone. He's written hundreds of feature articles, essays, film reviews, and book reviews for publications ranging from *Amazing Stories* and *The New England Journal of History* to BenBella's *King Kong is Back!* and *The Unauthorized X-Men*. His work has received five Origins Awards and an ENnie Award, and been nominated for the International Horror Guild Award and the Bram Stoker Award. Online at jameslowder.com.

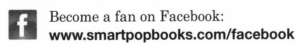

MORE COMICS TITLES

BATMAN UNAUTHORIZED
Vigilantes, Jokers, and Heroes in Gotham City
Edited by Dennis O'Neil

Eighteen leading writers explore Batman's motivations and actions, as well as those of his foes, and cover expansive territory from the cost (in cold hard cash) of being Batman to why Batman won't retire.

9781933771311 | Trade Paperback | $17.95 US/$19.95 CAN | February 2008

THE MAN FROM KRYPTON
A Closer Look at Superman
Edited by Glenn Yeffeth

Leading writers' in-depth analyses of the comics, films, and cartoons are at turns funny, philosophical, insightful, and personal, as they discuss, debate, and celebrate the legend of Superman.

9781932100778 | Trade Paperback | $17.95 US/$19.95 CAN | April 2006

THE PSYCHOLOGY OF SUPERHEROES
An Unauthorized Exploration
Edited by Robin S. Rosenberg, PhD

Almost two dozen psychologists get into the heads of today's most popular and intriguing superheroes to explore the inner workings our heroes usually only share with their therapists.

978-1933771311 | Trade Paperback | $17.95 US/$19.95 CAN | February 2008

THE UNAUTHORIZED X-MEN
SF and Comic Writers on Mutants, Prejudice and Adamantium
Edited by Len Wein

Science fiction and comic writers trace the X-Men series' evolution, challenge its metaphors, and draw from its truths about human nature and society in this exploratory look at the still-timely and often-revamped classic.

978-1932100747 | Trade Paperback | $17.95 US/$19.95 CAN | March 2006

WEBSLINGER
SF and Comic Writers on Your Friendly Neighborhood Spider-Man
Edited by Gerry Conway

Acclaimed writers of comics and science fiction explore the tangled web of vengeance, love, and loss woven by Spider-Man comics and films, from the friendly neighborhood of Peter Parker to Peter Parker's father issues.

978-1933771069 | Trade Paperback | $17.95 US/$19.95 CAN | February 2007